Darren Willing

Memoirs of a Stalker

Willing Publishing

Hermosa Beach, CA

Memoirs of a Stalker

Published by
Willing Publishing
P.O. Box 1411
Hermosa Beach, CA 90254
www.willingpublishing.com
willingpublishing@gmail.com

Edited by Ryan Huang and Darren Willing

Photography by Keenan Henson

Printed in the United States on acid-free paper

ISBN-13: 978-0-9815239-0-3
ISBN-10: 0-9815239-0-0

This book is dedicated to all those who would risk in hopes of a better tomorrow.

MEMOIRS OF A STALKER

You may encounter many defeats, but you must not be defeated.

—Maya Angelou

1

The Road to Hell...

There it was. I felt as though someone had shoved a grapefruit-sized ball of ice right down into the pit of my stomach. The twenty-nine year old "stalker" who lived in California and had been e-mailing his "victim" was me. I had made the nightly news and two newspapers. Damn... Of all the people in the world who could have acquired this dubious title, why did it have to be me? I would never harm a woman. I respect women. In fact, I respect them so much that the things too many men do to women on a regular basis disgust me intensely. People who know me know that I am ashamed to even be a man sometimes because of the behavior of many of the members of my sex. They take beautiful, special little girls and break their hearts. They lie. They cheat. They manipulate. They say that they love only to hang up the phone and crawl into another woman's bed. They make promises that they have no intention of keeping. They steal hope and trust. Nevertheless, I was the one who was feared; I was perceived as dangerous. In my fervent pursuit of this woman, I had crossed a line, and she had reacted in a way that I honestly did not believe she would. Maybe I just didn't want to. Finally, after five years of emotional hardship, the worst period of my life had reached its climax.

Perception is a funny thing. Two people can stand in the same place at the same time, watching the same event unfold and give two completely different accounts when asked to describe the event later. I think that out of all the things I've learned at this point, I have had the most trouble fully grasping this one. As a result, I've been largely misunderstood throughout my life: by strangers, acquaintances, classmates, and even my friends and family. My label as a stalker is also very much a result of this inability. Despite my denials that I have ever stalked anyone, or am even capable of such a thing, one particular woman and her friends would tell you otherwise. Perception…

This is my story. I want to share it with you so that you might understand who I truly am: so that you might know my strengths, my weaknesses, my insecurities, and most of all, my humanity. My hope is that you will be able to relate, if only in some small way. This is the story of how the shyest kid on the block lost his way, but somehow found the strength to carry on.

2

From the Beginning

I was born in the late seventies on a naval base in Naha, on the island of Okinawa, Japan. My father was in the Air Force and he had been stationed there for a two and one half year stint. Due to my size (nine pounds) and some other complications, I was delivered cesarean section. My grip on life was tenuous at first; I was a nice warm shade of yellow due to liver jaundice, and my lungs were compressed. Because of this, I lived the first two days of my life in an incubator. Luckily, my body was strong enough to get me through the first obstacle that life presented to me, and the doctors gave my parents the green light to take me home four days after my birth.

My childhood was largely uneventful. My older sister and I were raised in an amply sized house in a middle-class neighborhood. Except for almost drowning in a wash when I was about nine and a few concussions and broken bones, I managed to keep myself out of danger, for the most part. But I wouldn't say I was an average kid. I was taller than most, and I was good at just about anything I did, especially if I liked it. I did extremely well in school, and I excelled at sports; basketball was my favorite. However, there was one thing that

I was not good at, although I desperately wanted to be: social interaction. I was incredibly shy, and truthfully, I don't know why. I have generally believed that it was largely due to the way my mom coddled me. She was very protective: always petrified that I would hurt myself or get abducted. I can't blame my mother completely though because I think she treated my sister the same in that aspect; however, she seemed to be much braver than I was back then. For whatever reason, I suffered socially. Even as early as second grade, some of my classmates thought I was "conceited." As far as I can recall, this was the first time my perception about myself was at odds with that of the other people in my life. They thought that I was a snob because I didn't speak much. My lack of interaction wasn't the problem in and of itself; there were plenty of quiet kids. Unlike them, I was tall and well-groomed, athletic and smart. The other kids wanted to like me because of all of those qualities, but they took my reticence as me thinking they were below me and that I was too good to talk to them. The truth was that I felt just the opposite; I felt I was below them. They were more attractive, braver, and cooler. I thought that if I spoke to someone I didn't know without them talking to me first, they might start making fun of me for being a dork. I was terrified of older kids. In my mind, if I were to even speak around them, they would start smacking me around. (My mom made sure I was deathly afraid of physical injury, so I tried to avoid fights at all costs.) Try as I did to be better in social settings, the label stuck. The perception was that Darren was conceited.

Regardless of this particular problem, I had some close friends. My hometown was a very culturally diverse place to grow up. I had the privilege of being exposed to a lot of different types of people and their cultures, and it never made any difference to me what race my friends were. I happen to be of British (Scottish, Irish, English, and Welch) descent, but I had friends of every race and culture. As I have said before, I loved playing basketball, so I made a lot of black friends. I adopted many aspects of what I saw in their lives into my own personality. I listened to hip-hop and R&B and wore baggy jeans with Nike Airs.

From the Beginning

It was who I was. I don't want to be presumptuous about a culture by any means, but it has been my experience that African Americans are quite straightforward when it comes to opinions. They'll tell you what they think, for the most part. I have a lot of fond memories of eating dinner at my friend Maurice's home with his family. There was no shortage of opinions in that house. I only bring this up because I picked up a propensity to be opinionated from all my time around black culture. I still feel that it is a good thing, but when you already own the label of being conceited because you are shy, it isn't hard to imagine what will happen when you become opinionated without learning to be less shy in more intimate social situations. Bad mixture… But how can a kid who is just beginning to make sense of the world comprehend such a complex thing as social interaction? I couldn't then, and it wouldn't be until much later that I would start to understand.

My family life was complex; we were very dysfunctional. I'm sure you can figure out the cause. Money matters did a number on us. We were middle-class by income and living arrangements, but my parents had incredibly bad money management skills. All the fights that I can specifically remember them having (and there are quite a few) had something to do with money. After my father retired from the Air Force in 1987 because they were trying to send us to Turkey, he started his own electronics repair business. My mom really didn't work after I was about ten because of some issues she had with respecting authority, and my dad was stuck trying to support all four of us. His electronics repair business soon became a telecommunications management, repair, and installation business. His main client was a major financial organization, and he spent many years working twelve to fifteen hour days in a large credit card facility on the west side of town.

My father has great strength inside him. For all the garbage he had to put up with through the years, he did an incredible job of not displacing his inner turmoil on us. He was human, certainly, and made some mistakes; but given the magnitude of the pressure he faced, all I can do is applaud his fortitude. The way he handled those times have served as an example for me throughout my life.

Memoirs of a Stalker

My sister and I pretty much hated each other. I'm not talking about typical sibling hate though. For my part, I didn't give a damn whether she lived or died. I'm sure she'd say she didn't feel the same, but that certainly wouldn't explain why she was such a mean, jealous little girl. I would have beaten her into a coma a couple of times had my parents not been there to stop me. Somehow, we got through sixteen years of living together without any premature eulogies, to my parents' relief. Even afterwards, getting along for more than an hour or so seemingly always proved too much for us. As we have gotten older, we have been able to be somewhat more cordial to each other, but it can still be a struggle at times.

My mother and I were seemingly at odds from the start. She played favorites with my sister so blatantly that an outside observer could scarcely have any doubt that it was happening. My sister could (and did) get away with murder, but if I did anything wrong, my mom went nuts on me. My dad said it was because she held me to a higher standard than my sister. He said she was afraid that if she wasn't harder on me, I would end up like her two brothers (who systematically destroyed their own lives and were subsequently diagnosed with schizophrenia). I guess I can understand it now, but when I was just a kid, trying desperately to find a sense of self-worth, the way she treated me was intensely painful. By my pre-teen years, I had become opinionated and blunt, so at some point, things got nasty between us. Addressing my mother from the time I was about ten to the time I was eighteen, I'd bet I said the word "bitch" more than all the pimps in New York City in the same time period. She was asking for it anyhow! But there was that other side of her: the side that would send me money whenever I needed it while I was struggling to support myself through college (even if my father didn't think they could afford it); the side that worried about me eating enough; the side that always asked when I was coming home to visit. Although we had our troubles, and sometimes I didn't show it, I greatly appreciated having a mother like her.

From the Beginning

So I got through my young life. While it seemed harder for me than most of the people I knew, I understand that a lot of kids have it much worse, so I'm not complaining by any means. High school was a mixture of joy and pain. On one hand, I developed some really tight bonds with some friends that I am still close with to this day. On the other hand, I watched my dreams of NBA stardom die away because I wasn't mentally tough enough to compete at the high school level, even with my considerable physical talent. (I could slam dunk a basketball easily by the time I was sixteen and only five feet eleven inches tall.) Encouragingly though, I was still gaining confidence. My self-esteem had always been so fragile, but I had finally started to figure out that people would like me if I were friendly and genuine to them. Even the vast majority of people started to like me FOR my honesty and willingness to voice my opinions; and even though I was still very shy, I was getting better at dealing with it. When it was all said and done, I was looking forward to my future. I was going to college and then after that, who knew? Life was good, and I was learning and growing every day.

I attended college at the local university. Many of my friends were going away to "better" schools, but I ended up staying home because I didn't pull the grades I was capable of in high school. It really didn't matter to me because I felt I could learn just as much at my hometown school as my peers could learn at Harvard or Stanford or anywhere else. I went in determined to earn great grades and to get my life started right. My time there taught me how to turn off the tears that echoed in my head, and to devote myself to the things I wanted to accomplish. After a long five years and considerable change, including finding my confidence for the first time, I graduated with a solid G.P.A. More importantly, I gained some much-needed life experience.

I started dating the first woman I would ever love during my freshman year of college. Mara… She was wonderful. Through the years, we developed a strong, deep love for each other and we planned to be married one day. Had things gone a little differently, maybe we would have made it too. Even though we didn't, we remain close to this day; I'm sure we will for the rest of our lives.

It is quite an experience to be cruising along, confident and happy, when suddenly, your life comes apart at the seams. One second, you think you know where you're going and you've got a plan; the next second, you're flat on your back, kicking and flailing, just trying to turn over. Getting back on your feet isn't a priority because damage control is all you have the ability and resources to focus on. It happened to me. I guess the ironic thing is that I really did figure it was going to be smooth sailing for me at that point. I was in for the rudest of awakenings…

3

The Long, Hard Slap

As a career, I had chosen to become a dentist. As a result, a year after I graduated from college, I began four years of dental school. The school was located in a larger city in the United States. (My school will remain nameless as a courtesy to some of the people I will speak about in this book, and from now on, the city my school was in will be referred to as "Veiltown.") I had worked hard in college to get into the best dental school I could, and that had paid off with acceptance letters from three of the most highly respected programs in the entire nation. The program I attended had been my first choice because I liked the city it was in and thought it would be a fun place for the next chapter in my life. At the time, I was over five years into my relationship with Mara. She was going to attend law school, and our plan was to go to professional school in the same city, then get married afterwards. We had a choice between another large city and Veiltown, and I left it up to her. She picked Veiltown because the law school there had a higher national ranking than her other option. We packed up our stuff and headed into the future. I was excited to finally move away from home, as I had always felt that living in the same place for one's entire life was a bit shortsighted. The opportunity had finally come for me to get a different perspective. When we arrived in Veiltown, we rented a house where the two of us and my dog Jake settled in.

My experience in dental school can be summed up in one word: nightmare. There were two large reasons for this. The first reason had to do with coursework. I went in with expectations that becoming a dentist would be a challenge, for sure. However, I figured I would work hard, be dedicated, and graduate at the top of my class. After that, I planned to go on to become an oral and maxillofacial surgeon. To my dismay, I soon found that respect for students at my school was virtually non-existent as we were drowned with far too much information to get a handle on. My second problem can basically be called culture shock. I had built what I felt was a strong, honest, opinionated personality, and people had grown to like and respect me for it in my hometown. But in Veiltown, especially in a relatively small class of one hundred people, my particular brand of forthrightness was not in high demand. What was more, my confidence really seemed to piss people off.

Mara and I moved into a little house in a neighborhood in the northeast part of Veiltown about two weeks before I started my orientation. We set up our home with what we could afford: IKEA furniture and decorations. Those two weeks went by rapidly, and school soon started with a deafening "thud." Right at the start, I could see that there were major problems brewing in the building where I was to spend most of my time for the next four years.

4

Overload

For those who don't know, to become a dentist, one must learn about the
structure of the human body and how it functions. You don't have to become an
expert in anatomy and physiology, but you do have to know quite a bit. From
what I have heard, some years ago, the first two years of dental school used to be
exactly the same as the first two years of medical school. After that, a student
would learn dentistry in two years of classroom work and clinical training.
Nowadays, things have changed, but gross anatomy is still a requirement. I'm not
sure exactly how it works at other institutions, but at my school, the dental
students took gross anatomy with the medical students in a huge class that moved
at an extremely fast pace. Normally, dental students at my school did quite well
in gross anatomy, but that year there was something different about the course.
The medical school had made some changes in its curriculum. I'm not sure
exactly how it unfolded, but I know that the administration of the medical school
had decided to combine two ten-week gross anatomy courses into one thirteen-
week course. The two courses, gross anatomy of the trunk (basically everything
between the neck and the legs, excluding the arms) and gross anatomy of the

head and neck, were to be combined into one and taught at breakneck speeds. The director of the course had relayed an analogy that was often used about gross anatomy to us during the first weeks of school. He said that learning gross anatomy was like "trying to drink from a fire hose." I'm sure you get the implication. Now, imagine taking two sessions of "extreme water drinking" and squeezing them, basically, into the time it normally takes to do one. With already huge constraints on time, this was more like trying to drink from Niagara Falls. To be sure, both the dental students and the medical students were in for a tough challenge, but there was one key difference: the medical school administration had removed one course—a rather rigorous and fast-paced physiology class—from the schedule of the medical students. Did the dental school's administration do that for the dental students? Would I be asking if the answer was yes? Now, it has long been thought that first quarter dental students have it much harder than first quarter med students at that particular institution. The reason for this is that, along with a huge load of facts to memorize (as the med students also have), the dental students have the opportunity to learn to make teeth out of hot wax with small metal instruments and a Bunsen burner. The grading in that class was, in a word, ludicrous. It took loads of time for most of us to do C work. There were some who had a knack for "waxing," as it was called, but most of us struggled. If not for the written tests, I would have been near failing. The point is that we already had about as much as we could handle on our plates without the extra ten-week course squeezed in. But that isn't all of it.

In past years, the dental school had allowed anyone in the program to take a challenge exam for the histology (the study of living tissues) course given during the first quarter of school. If you passed (and most did), you could eliminate histology from your schedule. Usually, out of the one hundred people in the dental school class, ninety to ninety-five would test out of histology. Some brave souls with a real hunger for knowledge (or perhaps something else) would not challenge the course and therefore keep it on their schedules. That year, along with not removing another course so we could keep up with our all-consuming

12

gross anatomy course, our administrators had decided that the students were being cheated if they were allowed to challenge the histology course without having taken histology in college. Let's not forget that there was a special "oral histology" course designed specifically for dental students later in the year. We would be taught all the histology we would need to be dentists in that course. I guess our administrators were too busy worrying about standardized test scores and how the students weren't doing well enough in the histology section to realize that we already had way too much work; they made a rule that said only those who had taken histology and passed it in college could test out of it. Instead of ninety-two out of one hundred people not taking the course, we ended up with ninety-two out of one hundred actually TAKING the course. For those eight fortuitous souls who had taken histology in college, the quarter was challenging, but not nearly as bad as what the other ninety-two of us went through.

So we started what ended up being the most ridiculously stressful and soul-sucking academic experience most of us had ever been through. The toll it took was obvious within the first few weeks. I had spoken to many of the people in the class above us about how their first-year experience had gone. They didn't have favorable things to say, for sure. Evidently, by the ninth or tenth week, quite a few people had broken down crying from the pressures of trying to pass all of their classes. (They had two fewer courses than we did.) In the third week of school, many of my classmates decided that they couldn't hold in their tears for another seven weeks. That was followed by all sorts of physiological problems. One of my classmates had half his face go numb. Another fainted and had to be taken to the emergency room. Yet another had blood in his stool. Stress is a mother... I myself developed a lovely twitch in my left upper eyelid that was present much of the time. It isn't so easy to study when you can barely see out of one eye due to rapidly fluttering eyelashes. I don't think I am overstating anything when I say that something was wrong.

5

No Suffering in Silence

That quarter was as stressful as anything academic I had ever experienced—even more so. At first, I thought that I just needed to work harder and I would adjust as soon as I got myself going. After all, I had been out of school for about a year and a half. (I had finished my requirements for dental school at the very end of college, so I couldn't apply for admission for the upcoming year.) I knew from my B.A. in psychology that people get better at learning the more they do it, and periods of inactivity will take away the mental sharpness that has been gained through studying. I was hopeful that a little effort would get rid of the rust and I would soon be mentally sharp once again. After a while, I was studying every minute that I possibly could. I would only take breaks to eat and sleep—and believe me, I felt guilty even doing that. Only on Friday nights would I put down the books for a while and relax with Mara. She would cook us dinner, and we would watch <u>America's Funniest Videos</u>. I knew that I had to have some sort of reprieve from the unimaginable grind that I was being forced to go through, and laughing with my girlfriend always seemed to help. After the show was over, I would go to bed early and sleep as much as I needed to recuperate from an exhausting week. I would generally wake up around ten AM Saturday and go right back to studying or making wax teeth. Sunday would be the same. Occasionally, we would go somewhere or hang out with my classmate Brendan and his girlfriend Ilia. When we did, I felt so guilty afterwards that it was probably more counterproductive than productive. At any rate, I was soon pushing as hard as I could, and I was falling further behind each day. How could this be? I knew just how capable I was (especially when I put effort into things), but I absolutely could not keep up. I was failing quizzes in Gross Anatomy. FAILING! I had never failed at any academic pursuit that I had put so much effort into before. In the past, it had been unlikely that I would get less than a B on any test, even with little to no effort. My waxing grades were piss-poor as well.

Our class officers were working to alleviate our suffering through the proper channels. The president Lee was especially active. Even so, before we knew it, we were eight weeks into the twelve-week quarter and the faculty had done nothing to help us. Then one day, I lost it. I was trying to study for gross anatomy on a Sunday afternoon. Mara was out and I had some one hundred and fifty pages of our gigantic anatomy textbook to read for a heavily weighted quiz the next day. I read for a couple of hours and got about twenty pages into my assignment. I was exhausted, so my eyes were trying to close with every word I read. I tried to focus, but my brain was malfunctioning and attempting to shut itself down. It was tired of reading and memorizing and learning in general, and it was telling me in no uncertain terms, "Enough!" I closed the book and just sat there for a moment. I thought to myself, "How can they be this disrespectful? There is no way we can keep up with this workload. What the hell are they thinking?" As my mind wrapped around the situation, I felt an incredible anger building up inside of me. My fury grew stronger and stronger, and all of a sudden, I found myself ripping the textbook in half down the center of its spine. Then I threw both pieces as hard as I could into the box spring (that we were getting ready to throw away) which was propped against the wall in the living room. I grabbed a decorative wooden framed mirror from the wall and broke it over my knee, then tossed it to the ground. I stood there, just shaking with rage, wondering what I was going to do. "What if I fail out of dental school? What then?" I wondered. I tried to calm myself for a minute, and when I stopped shaking, I realized that the time for waiting was over. If there was one thing I knew how to do, it was struggle for what I believed in. I was a fighter. I knew what had to be done.

I sat down at the computer in the dining room and began writing an e-mail to the highest authority in the school, the dean. Screw the system and proper channels. The abuse had to end. I was very clear in my letter to the Dean about how I and many of my classmates felt about the way we were being treated. I felt that it was absolutely inexcusable to overload us the way they had and that it spoke poorly about the school itself. I told her that if someone didn't do something about it soon, I was going to quit. It wasn't a threat—just the truth. I didn't work so hard as an undergraduate to be treated so unfairly in dental school. I told her about one of the members of our class fainting and how extremely stressed out many of us were. However, I did make sure to make it clear that I wasn't speaking for the entire class. I hadn't actually talked to anyone who was happy about the situation, but I was sure that there would be at least some people who didn't feel that anything needed to be changed. I sent the letter off to the dean and also a copy of it to each of my classmates. It did pertain to them as well, not just to me. Afterwards, I resigned not to study anymore that day. Screw the quiz. I needed to rest.

The dean responded quickly. She e-mailed me back the next day and told me that she hadn't realized how most of the class really felt about the situation. She promised that she would do something about it as quickly as possible. I was relieved to see that the members of our administration actually had at least one human being amongst them. The dean called a meeting after school the next day where we would discuss the issues at hand.

Lee came to talk to me and express some displeasure with what I had done. He was concerned that my speaking out without going through the proper channels would give our class a reputation as a group that "didn't play by the rules" and didn't have a coherent, unified voice. While I told him that I understood what he was getting at and that I appreciated his candor, I also told him very frankly that he wasn't working fast enough. A lot of us were tired of waiting; if something wasn't done immediately, quite a few people were going to fail at least one course. He was frustrated with me (I could plainly see), but we agreed to disagree and went about our business. I did gain a large amount of respect for Lee that day. He handled things very professionally and with an open mind. Alan, another classmate of mine, met me in the hallway outside of one of our classes and told me that he didn't like the fact that I had sent a letter to the dean. He felt I had acted rashly, and he knew quite a few people, including himself, that didn't have any problem with the workload; they didn't see any need to change the schedule. He also said that I made it seem like I was speaking for the entire class when I sent the letter. I told him that he should reread it because I had specifically stated that I was not speaking for the entire class. I also told him that he and some other extremely talented people in our class may not have been having trouble with the load, but most of us were. Everyone was there to become a dentist, and it would not serve the class as a whole or the school if a large portion of us failed or only learned the material at a surface level and passed on a sharply skewed curve. We didn't argue about it for long, and we both kept our cool, but that incident set a tone for our interactions in the future. It would be a while yet before we would figure each other out.

At the class meeting, we all had a nice little discussion. I was very assertive as I expressed my feelings and defended my actions to a small band of my classmates, including Alan, who thought that no changes needed to be made to our schedule. I couldn't figure out what planet that group of people was from, but I wanted to actually LEARN what was being presented to me (not just gloss it over and forget what little bit I was able to glean from the chaos). Fortunately, those who dissented were the minority. Most of the class agreed with my point of view and shared stories with the Dean about the stresses they were dealing with and how upset they felt. A couple of people even got teary-eyed. At the end of the meeting, we had a vote; surprisingly to me, there were about fifteen people who thought that our schedule was fine the way it was. Luckily, the overwhelming majority of people wanted a change, so we agreed to remove histology from our schedule in order to make time to focus on more important subjects. All we had to do was write a little paper explaining how a certain type of tissue in the body worked. I thought that I had done a good thing by speaking up and that most of my classmates would appreciate it. Indeed, a fair amount of them thanked me openly for having the courage to voice my concerns. Despite that fact, I had started to build a prevailing perception of myself with my actions in relation to that issue. Before I knew what was going on, that perception would grow into an untrue, twisted monster.

6

In Stride

The removal of histology from our schedule helped most of us to pass all of our classes. If I remember correctly, two or three people didn't pass the final exam in Gross Anatomy. Unfairly, they had to re-study the material during the next quarter, which was considerably lighter as far as course load went. Then they retook the final exam. In spite of the extra hassle, they all passed. My G.P.A. for the first quarter had been much lower than I was used to, and I was upset with the whole situation. I felt that I had been cheated out of valuable knowledge. If our faculty hadn't been so careless and inconsiderate, I would have gotten much more out of the first quarter. When it came down to it, I wanted to learn as much as I could in dental school and go on to become an oral surgeon. I felt a responsibility to the people I would be treating in the future to know as much as possible. When second quarter came, I was determined to do better.

With the stress of the overloaded first quarter over, I began to feel somewhat more myself. I had always found that I learned more when I participated actively in class. Just listening to lectures and taking notes had never captured my attention that well, so whenever I could, I would ask questions and offer my own insights in relation to the topics we were learning about. As it turns out, this sort of behavior was something that a large number of the people in my class didn't like. They felt I was wasting their time and that I should wait until after class to ask my questions and discuss things with professors. Annoyingly, I wouldn't find out directly from the people who disliked my participation. I would only find out "through the grapevine." Lee and I had come to like and respect each other quite a bit by the middle of the year, and he started to clue me in on the popular notion that was beginning to surface about me. A few people had come directly to him and said that they thought something needed to be done about me. What?! "Needed to be done?" What the hell did that mean? Lee didn't agree. He thought I contributed a lot to class and that my questions and insights made things more interesting. Contrarily, there were some people who just wanted to get out of class as soon as possible. My participation, in their minds, prevented that. Weren't we at school? Weren't we supposed to WANT to learn? Truthfully, knowing that only made me angry and retaliatory at first. My attitude was: "Screw them. If the teacher lets me participate, I'm going to participate. I'm paying for this, after all." I just kept doing what I was doing, not caring at all if it made anyone mad. What did it matter to me if small-minded people like that disliked me anyhow? To some extent, I even started to like the idea that my actions were making them angry.

Because I like to relate to people by talking about things that they and I have in common, I would often talk about school and grades and such with my classmates. It seemed like the thing to do, being as we were all suffering through the same trials. Alan didn't like that fact though, and he let me know about it in front of the others a couple of times: "Why do you want to talk about school all the time? There are other things in life besides this, you know." I had also continued to be vocal when it came to expressing myself about how we were being mistreated and overworked. (Even after first quarter was done, the workload was still far beyond reasonable.) Alan openly criticized me for complaining too much. I didn't really know how to reply to the things he said to me or his tone. It was clear that he didn't like me very much, and I really couldn't understand why. From what he said, it seemed to me that he thought I was trying to compare myself to everyone else; he thought that by talking about school and grades, I wanted to create an opportunity to brag about how smart I was. He was so far off from the truth. I was just a forward person, and I was curious about how other people were doing and coping; I wanted to vent to them and to let them vent to me in return. If they did well, I wanted to congratulate them. If they didn't do so well, I wanted to encourage them. When I complained, I was just trying to relate and share my pain with people who I thought were suffering through the same troubles. Alan took it as arrogance and whining, and so did quite a few others. Naturally, the way that Alan and I interacted put me on the defensive.

Butting heads with Alan was troublesome, but it was nothing compared to the way one of my other classmates got under my skin. His name was Mason. I met him during our first week of school. At the time, he seemed to be a decent guy. Within another week, he completely turned my initial appraisal of him around. At my dental school, during the first two years, students spent a significant amount of time in a simulation laboratory. That was where all of the technical aspects of dentistry were practiced in preparation for the move into the clinics during third year. The room was set up with workbenches arranged around twelve or thirteen pentagons and the students were assigned to pentagons alphabetically. Mason and I were two seats away from each other at the same pentagon. I remember the day my troubles with him began. It was Friday of the second week of school and we were in the lab for our first waxing session in the dental anatomy course. Our assignment that day was to wax half of an upper central incisor (one of the "two front teeth"). While we worked, the instructors would come around and talk to us, giving advice on technique and trying to learn a bit about us. As I waxed, one of the instructors came over to me. He had noticed that I was wearing the football jersey and hat of our university. Starting up the conversation, he stated, "Somebody's from around here." As soon as he said it, I heard an effeminate male voice from the other side of the pentagon say, "Uh, yeah. He's definitely not from around here." As I tried to keep my focus on the instructor and our conversation, all I could think was, "What the hell is THAT supposed to mean?" I hadn't even started to alienate myself from the rest of the class yet. If it had happened later, I might have been able to understand it, but as it was, this guy had no reason to take such a disrespectful tone about me. I managed to have a nice chat with the instructor until he moved on, but I was confused as to why Mason would say something like that. After that, I decided to pay close attention to the way he conducted himself.

Subsequently, I noticed some very disturbing things about Mason. He was very critical of others and had an opinion about everyone's value. In lectures, if one of our classmates asked a question that he deemed to be less than useful, Mason would sigh audibly and roll his eyes. He was a hard worker, for sure, and I at least respected him for that, but he was also deceitful. Sometimes he would have two different stories concerning the same issue. For example, I once heard him telling someone that he had played semi-professional soccer. When they asked why he had not continued on with it, he said that he had suffered a knee injury that ended his career. I was conversing with him a few days later, and I asked him why he had left soccer and come to dental school. He told ME that he just got tired of soccer. ??? What? I caught him running that sort of game at least two more times. I guess he didn't know that I was paying attention. Besides the deceit, the other things he did seemed pretty arrogant. I know that a lot of people in my class thought the same about me, but I never did the things he did. The upsetting thing about that was that it seemed that a lot of people liked him, but didn't like me. I didn't get it at all. It was like many of my classmates would just turn a blind eye to the things he did. Then again, quite a few people disliked him rather passionately, so at least the whole class wasn't oblivious. Nonetheless, there was a more mature and sensitive part of me that held onto the idea that I just misunderstood Mason. Even though my instincts were strongly in favor of hating him by mid-year, I did my best to try and get past it.

In Stride

I was working extremely hard by the middle of the second quarter, but I didn't mind because I felt like I was beginning to get a hold of everything. Unlike first quarter, my efforts were being rewarded with good grades, and I could actually do what was being asked of me. Notwithstanding, I was still working every minute that I could. I still hadn't taken much time to have any kind of social life because I figured I was tough enough to go without while I focused on my career goals. I should have known myself better than that. Even so, Mara was there, working hard at her law school coursework. It was a comfort to come home and spend each evening with her, even if we were both studying. She had a lot fewer credits than I did, so she would usually make dinner while I shoved page after page of information into my mind. We would eat and chat, and then we would both get back to our duties.

I would study with Brendan sometimes and also with a guy that I had gone to college with named Eddie. Eddie and I had almost all of our science classes together in college, and we had even lived together for a few months during my senior year. We were about equally intelligent and motivated, so we were pretty productive together. For a time, that little bit of social interaction served me just fine, as I had aspirations to tend to. It wouldn't be long before I would need something more.

I did very well on my finals that quarter, and my G.P.A. improved quite a bit. Most importantly, I knew I had learned much more than I had during first quarter. When third quarter started, I was in full stride. I was working so much harder than I ever had in my life, and my abilities had finally caught up to my effort level. I did well on every assignment we had; I even got an A on an assignment where we had to wax-up two crowns. Midterms were to be rigorous, with seven large tests in ten days. I put my head down and bashed my way through them. After each and every test, I walked out of the room knowing, without any doubt, that I had gotten an A. The last test was in a class called "Functional Occlusion," which concerned how the teeth contact each other and work harmoniously with the muscles and other factors so as to perform their duties and not damage each other (a little complicated, I know). That particular course was run by a professor who was notorious for his difficult exams. Few people, if any, got A's on his written tests. He had been the course director of the waxing course during the first quarter, and we had taken only one written test: the final. I managed to get a ninety percent on that, so I wasn't intimidated by his midterm for this class. Maybe I should have been. The test was on a Friday and I had, out of necessity, neglected to study for it until the night before. I had no choice but to stay up all night studying the huge mountain of information that was to be covered. I was absolutely spent when it came time to put the pencil to the paper, but I focused and went to work.

I doubt that I will ever take a more difficult or more stressful test. Explaining that nightmare would be a waste of time because I'm not even sure I understood it fully. I worked up until the very last possible second, checking and rechecking all of my answers because more than anything, the professor's testing format was designed to induce mistakes by the student. I knew the material though, so there was no way on earth I was going to let him win by defeating myself through inattention. I wanted to collapse after I turned it in, but I knew that my paper was an A. There was no way it couldn't be.

That afternoon, we were supposed to go to the simulation lab to practice adjusting teeth on a stone model. I went and did a little bit, but mostly I just sat there exhausted, chatting with some of the instructors and other students. I didn't get much done, but I could make it up during the next week. I had worked my tail off. It was, without a doubt, the most intense period of focused effort I had ever been through. More than anything, I needed to sleep.

7

Prelude to Affliction

I got home at around five o'clock that night. Mara made dinner, but I wasn't up for watching <u>America's Funniest Videos</u>. I went to sleep as soon as I finished eating, around six PM. I woke up at eleven AM the next day.

When I awoke, I could tell that something was wrong... very wrong. I felt a large void inside of me. In the past, giving a great effort at schoolwork and being rewarded with high marks had always made me feel good. I knew that I had gotten an A on every one of the seven tests I had just taken, but I didn't feel happy about it. I didn't feel happy at all. It seemed that I had given too much of myself, and for what? I felt lonely and dejected. Who cared if I got good grades? I knew what I was capable of, and I didn't need to prove it to myself just for the sake of proving it. Why was I working so hard? Suddenly, the thought occurred that I didn't have any great passion for dentistry. There were a million things I could think of that would be more fun than this career (although most not as high paying). After a few minutes of contemplation, it became clear to me: I spilled my guts out for those tests...those stupid tests. In return, all I had was sadness. I had no social life to speak of, and I was never at ease because all I could think about was my responsibility to "do my best." I wanted to quit. Even so, I knew that actually being a dentist would be very different from dental school, so I was prudent and didn't make any rash decisions. Besides, I already had fifty thousand dollars worth of student loans to pay back, and I didn't know how I would do that if I didn't become a dentist.

The emptiness I felt was a bear to deal with, but I was a soldier. I kept going, hoping I could work it all out in my mind. I went back to school the next week with very little desire to even pay attention at all. However, I was a good student. It was hard for me to just quit being that, and there was nothing good that would come of me giving up. Despite that, I was pretty out of it. The mounting criticism from my classmates had really started to tick me off, especially considering that most of them didn't have the guts to tell me to my face. There was an incident in which I was trying to get clarification about what a lecturer was saying because she seemingly interchanged a particular term for a closely related one. It confused me, so I asked her what she meant and explained my understanding of the two terms to her. She wasn't offended, but apparently, many members of my class felt that I was trying to "show her up." It was even one of the topics at a class meeting and my classmates discussed it for fifteen minutes or so. (Of course, I didn't go to class meetings because I didn't care to at that point.) Par for the course, none of the people who had a problem with it ever talked to me about it directly. I only found out from Lee after the fact.

One day, a few weeks before the end of the quarter, we were all in a lecture hall preparing for our periodontics class (a class concerning the gums). Summertime was nearing rapidly, so people were anxious to be done with first year and to get onto the four-month vacation. (That would be the only such vacation of our entire time there.) At any rate, the room was loud with people conversing and carrying on. When the professor tried to start class, he was unsuccessful at getting everyone's attention. He tried a second time, but the talking didn't get any quieter. I could see that he was getting frustrated and it made me a bit angry. I couldn't understand why my class was being so disrespectful. I took it upon myself to help the professor get class started. First, I tried to "shush" the class. They quieted down for a few seconds, but then returned to what they were doing. I tried again—this time, a little louder. The noise level dipped slightly and immediately returned to a level even higher than it had been at before. The professor was very obviously getting angry, as I could see by his expression. I tried again. This time, I clapped my hands together three times, and I did it rather loudly. No one even heard it! That was it. I was at the front of the room, so I turned around and yelled at the class, "Would y'all get the hint?! Shut up!" Utter silence. That was better. I couldn't believe that a group of supposed "future professionals" was acting so juvenile. I returned my gaze to the front of the room, and class started.

I guess I sort of let out a lot of my frustration on my classmates that day. It was hard not to. My dejection with school and its coursework had drawn my attention to my social life and how it was lacking. I felt like very few of my classmates liked me. It seemed that many of them would be nice to my face and act like everything was all fine and good, but then they would talk trash about me when my back was turned. What was worse, save for one or two people, I didn't know exactly who didn't like me because of their duplicity; I had little idea who was saying those things about me to Lee. The class's rudeness to our professor gave me enough of a reason to lash out, and I made a big mistake that day. My participation in class, my forwardness, my honesty about how I felt, my complaining about the way the school treated us, the confident way in which I carried myself, and my intentional lack of social interaction already rubbed many of my classmates the wrong way. Along with all of that, my little outburst gave a lot of people enough justification to not like me, and I would spend the rest of my time in dental school working against the popular perception: Darren was an arrogant jerk.

Mason was walking on thin ice with me by the end of the year. I had taken an opportunity to try and clear up my unfavorable perception of him one night in the lab. We were talking, and I decided to ask him why he gave me a different story about his soccer career than he had given to other people. He said he didn't know what I was talking about. Then I asked him why he had made that comment about me not being from the area during the second week of school. He didn't remember saying it, or so he said. Why was I not surprised? The conversation was my attempt to reach out to Mason and to understand him better, but he stonewalled me. I left the lab feeling pretty angry with him. After that, I kept noticing him being his normal, self-absorbed, arrogant self in class. It made me want to... I'm getting riled up just writing about it.

When finals came for that quarter, I barely studied. I was much more concerned with figuring out how to make myself feel happy again. While everyone else was getting ready for all of the tests we were about to take, I was out playing basketball at the park near my house or lifting weights. My exercise routine had been sporadic due to the hectic schedule, and I was tired of not being in good shape. I resigned never to neglect to exercise again for any reason that still left me with some control.

Blowing off my studies was freeing. It wasn't too hard to do either. As the year progressed, I had gradually come to grips with the fact that most of the stuff we learned during the first year was absolutely useless information. I mean seriously, who in God's name cares how long the average central incisor is? And that whole idea about becoming an oral surgeon? To hell with that. I wasn't going to go to MORE school after I finished with that horror show.

I did fine on final exams and even jumped up quite a bit in the class rankings. It didn't make me happy. On top of my dejection with school and my feelings of isolation, Mara and I had started to grow apart by then as well. We were communicating less and less each day. I wondered how we could continue on and get married with me feeling so unhappy in our relationship. I could see that she wasn't happy either. For so long, she had been the most important and best thing in my life; to add to my troubles, I was losing her too. I just tried to hang on the best I could. I promised her at the beginning of our relationship that I would give her all I had, and I meant it. I would stay until every possible option was exhausted.

8

Deeper and Deeper

Near the end of the school year, Jake had begun to get extremely lonely during
the daytime while we were gone. Of course, dogs are pack animals and need
social interaction to be happy, especially when they are young. Jake had decided
that he was tired of being left out in the backyard with no one to play with. He
began whining and yelping loudly, to the chagrin of our neighbors. A couple of
them even left anonymous, nasty notes on our door. We had to do something, and
the only plausible idea seemed to be to get another dog to keep Jake company;
we went to the local animal shelter and picked out a skinny, one year old Akita
mix. We named him Percival, but he quickly became Percy, for short. He had
been out in the forest near the animal shelter for a while when they found him,
and he was in pretty sickly shape, with large patches of his fur missing and
terrible breath, even for a dog. He was very well behaved though, especially
inside, and we could tell that someone else had owned him before. He was also a
little jittery, ducking his head at any sudden movement. We became relatively
certain that he had been abused; maybe he even ran away because of it. Percy and
Jake were instant best friends, and Mara and I loved him immediately. He

wouldn't have to worry about his owners abusing him anymore. As the days passed, he put on weight and his fur began to grow back in. Soon he was healthy and strong.

When the summer came, I went to see my family. When I was a couple of years into college, my father had dissolved his company. He and my mother then sold the house and moved to Nampa, Idaho (a small farming town just east of Boise). They lived off savings for a while, but my father eventually landed a job doing information technology for the government. It was a good change for him to get away from the pressure of the private sector, and he and my mother had bought some land and started a small farm of sorts. I had not seen my family in over a year, and they wanted me to come and visit. In order to be closer to my parents, my sister and her family had also moved to Idaho. Kaleb, her son, wanted to see me as well. He also wanted me to bring Jake. I had first gotten Jake when I was living with my parents in Nampa for a short period before dental school. Kaleb (typical of a little boy) loved playing with him. I packed Jake into the car, and we headed off on the long drive for my parents' house. Mara was busy with some volunteer work for law school, so she stayed at home.

On the way to Idaho, I stopped on the side of the freeway to let Jake do his business and stretch out his legs every few hours. He was a very active dog, and he would often get tired of being cramped up in the car. On the last of our stops, I remember feeling very nervous about all of the cars whizzing by. Terrible "what ifs" ran through my head. What if Jake somehow got off the leash? What if it broke? What if he ran out onto the freeway and got hit? Just thinking about it almost made me tear up. I held tightly to him and got him back into the car as soon as I could. Then we continued on to my parents' place. As we drove, I felt uneasy. I didn't know why, but I was strongly concerned for Jake. I had a really bad feeling.

We pulled into my parents' home at around one-thirty AM, and after I talked to my mother for a few minutes, Jake and I retired to our bedroom. He slept on the bed next to me, as he had always done when we lived there. At about

34

seven AM, Jake heard my father rustling around and decided that he wanted to go out and play. I got out of bed and we went into the living room to see my dad. Jake was so excited to get outside and run around in his old stomping grounds, and my dad promised he would keep an eye on him (as he used to when I had first brought Jake home). The main road was about one hundred yards away from the front of the house, and Jake had known not to go near it when he was younger; I made sure of that with the proper loud yelling. With my dad supervising, I figured I didn't need to worry about anything that morning, although I still felt uneasy. I should have gone out with him… Instead, I grabbed him by his face and kissed him on his forehead as he stood in front of me anxiously awaiting my "okay" to go out and play. My dad opened the back door, and Jake took off. That was the last time I ever saw him alive.

I went back to bed and fell asleep within minutes. The way I woke up was one of the most unpleasant experiences I have ever been through. The window of my room was open, and at nine-thirty, I was ripped from my slumber by the sound of my father yelling my name in a frantic and anguished tone that I had never heard from him before. As soon as my eyes opened, I knew… Jake was dead. I looked out the window to see my father running towards it with my beautiful puppy's body hanging limp in his arms. In his right hand was Jake's collar, which had been broken at the plastic clasp by the impact of the vehicle. I didn't know what to do, so I got up and went outside. It had really happened. Jake had run out into the road and been hit by a car. He died, and it was my fault… all my fault. I asked myself why I hadn't just stayed up and gone outside with him.

When I got outside, my father met me with the most desperately apologetic look on his face. I took Jake from him and buried my face in his fur. As I held him, sobbing, the only other thing I could do was apologize silently to him for what I had done. I had been the worst kind of irresponsible, and he, not I, had paid the ultimate price. When I rescued Jake from the animal shelter, he was only three months old and very ill. He had just been neutered, and when we arrived home, I put him down on top of a blanket on the floor of my room and lay next to him until he fell asleep. Once he was sleeping, I crept out of the room silently, only to return ten minutes later when he awoke crying at the realization that I wasn't there. I had nursed him back to health and watched him grow, and I had loved him with all of my heart. He brought so much joy to my life. But his time had passed, and there was no one to blame but me. I killed him, and it tore my heart out to put him into the ground that day.

My father blamed himself, but I made sure he knew that I didn't hold him responsible for what had happened. It didn't make him feel any better. Predictably, my mother bawled her head off in her melodramatic, almost artificial way. After a minute, I went inside and called Mara. When she answered, I could barely get a word out. Her voice was concerned as she asked me what was wrong. When I told her that Jake was gone, she burst into tears. That made me cry even more. She asked me what happened, and I explained how I had messed up and let Jake go outside without me. She forgave me right then and there, I know. Forgiving myself wouldn't prove so easy. Then there was Percy. What would he think when I came back without his best friend? We had owned him long enough to know that he was not going to react well to what had happened. We made a decision that I should go to the animal shelter that day and adopt another dog, so as to speed up the adjustment process and get Percy accustomed to his new playmate as quickly as possible.

I went to the animal shelter in Boise that afternoon and picked up a nine-month-old, red waif of a dog with floppy ears and a regal face. As I walked by his cage, he whimpered and pawed at the lock. In my heart-broken state, that little gesture was enough for me, so I adopted him. Mara and I named him Rusty, for the color of his fur.

After eating dinner with my sister and her family at their home that evening (and explaining to my nephew where Jake had gone), I went to sleep back at my parents' house. In the morning, I woke up early and left for Veiltown. I had never had any great love for Nampa as it was, and now just being there hurt terribly. I wanted to go home and be with my girlfriend and Percy. The ride back was long, and the only thing I could think about was Jake. Rusty behaved well and didn't go to the bathroom in the car. That was a plus. When I walked through the door of the house with a strange new dog, Percy (who had excitedly come to the door to greet Jake and me) was not happy. He growled aggressively at Rusty, and I grabbed him by the face and told him "No!" sternly. Then I looked up at Mara. As I stood up, she put her arms around my head and shoulders and pulled me tightly to her. I began to cry as soon as I felt her. "I wanna wake up now," I told her. She just rocked me back and forth until I was done sobbing. For the first time in quite a while, I felt close to her.

As the dogs adjusted to each other and I dealt with the pain, I still had to acknowledge the fact that I was going to have to go back to school in the fall. I tried so hard to figure out a way to not go, or at least to be able to quit soon. We had almost four months of vacation, and I was determined to find something else to do with my life besides dentistry. I thought about applying for the CIA or joining the military and becoming a fighter pilot or trying out for an NBA team. I wanted my life to be exciting, and dentistry was just not cutting it at that point. I wasn't lacking confidence in my abilities, and I knew that if I wanted it badly enough, I had the physical skills to make an NBA team. I decided that trying out for the NBA was the most plausible course of action. I just had to get my body ready and my skills honed. I started training. I lifted weights regularly and I started running to get my legs into shape for the hell I was about to put them through. After about three weeks of running three or four times per week, I began to train with Strength Shoes. For those of you who don't know, Strength Shoes are a training system that focuses on calf strength and endurance. I won't go into the details, but I knew from using them previously that they really worked when it came to improving speed, quickness, power, and jumping ability. The first time I did the full routine with the shoes, I increased my vertical leap by some ten inches.

The routine was harsh, calling for three days out of the week and involving all sorts of movements including sprinting, jumping, skipping, and the like. I needed to work as hard as I possibly could, so I bought a weight suit and did the routine while carrying thirty extra pounds of weight. My sadness and regret made it difficult to be motivated, but nonetheless, I got started. Things went fine at first, and I was pushing myself to exhaustion each time out. I would go so hard that by the time I finished, I was usually wheezing audibly due to exercise induced asthma. I was proud of my efforts and planned to keep pushing myself until I got where I wanted to be. However, at the start of the sixth week out of twelve, I pulled a muscle in my back so badly that I was in bed for three days, unable to walk. That ended that. By the time I got healed and could start back up again, I wouldn't be able to complete the training before it was time to return to school.

Next, I seriously entertained the idea of joining the military as a pilot. The competition was supposedly fierce, but that didn't scare me at all; I could do it if I wanted to. After thinking long and hard about it though, I decided that I didn't want to kill people for a living. The CIA would have been a good option and more in line with my morality, but generally only ex-military made the cut to be field agents (and CIA field agents kill people too). I decided that it wasn't worth the risk to try, especially considering the fifty thousand dollars of debt I was already carrying from my first year in dental school. I guessed I would have to continue on. Despite that fact, I made a promise to myself that I wasn't going to be a dentist forever. It would only be a temporary career.

At the end of the first school year, I had been so irritated with Mason and his general method of conducting himself that I started to vent my frustrations to other people in the class. I went to an end-of-the-year party that Lee threw, just to try and start mending some fences with my classmates. At the end of the night, I gave a ride home to a guy named Randy. Randy was a little older than most of the class, and he was a standup guy. I figured that because he was such a good person, he might understand my frustrations with Mason's deceitfulness and arrogance. We talked about it for a while, and I ended up telling him that if I were five years younger, I would have probably put Mason in the hospital by then. He listened and seemed to understand, but I found out a few weeks later that he had told Mason about what I said, fearing that I might try to harm him. Once I knew that, I decided that I should just put an end to all of it. I wasn't actually going to hurt the guy, but I did dislike him pretty strongly. I knew that wasn't really acceptable either, so I told a mutual acquaintance of mine and Mason's that I wanted to bury the hatchet and just put the past behind us. He set up a phone conversation between the two of us, and Mason and I talked for probably an hour. It seemed that Mason wasn't so bad after all. He told me that he didn't mean any harm with the things he did, but it sometimes appeared that way. He said that he used to be very conceited and had a tendency to look down on people when he was in high school. He felt he had improved quite a bit since then, although he knew he still had work to do. He was also sorry if he had offended me in any way. I was happy to accept his apology, and I apologized for my part in the matter. I thought we were going to be able to put it all behind us. I was even hoping that we might become friends in the future. Time would tell.

9

Round Two

When school started back up I was absolutely not happy. Second year was
thought to be even more rigorous than first year. (As if they hadn't treated us
disrespectfully enough!) Our schedule called for us to be in class at seven-thirty
every single morning. We had some seven-thirty classes during first year, but not
every day! What a joke. My motivation was in ruin. I thought about Jake often,
and I would sometimes wake up in the middle of the night feeling nauseated
about losing him. My regret made it even harder for me to care about school.
Then there was the fact that I was unsure about what I was even doing there. That
sure didn't help me to peel my under-slept body out of bed every morning. I
would go to class and sit through mind-numbing lectures while having trouble
keeping my eyes open. Of course, if I would have been able to participate in
class, the lectures would have been much more bearable. But my classmates had
made it clear that they didn't want me to do that the year before, and I was really
tired of dealing with all of the poor opinions that circulated regarding me. Feeling
ostracized is a lot easier to deal with if you have a purpose—if you have a clear
view of your future and you are working towards it. I was in limbo. I didn't know

where my future was going to take me. That weighed on my mind enough without everyone in my class hating me. Without my classmates' permission to participate, I would sit in class and nod off as the lecturers dumped more and more information on top of us. After a while, I stopped even trying to fight the urge to sleep.

Even though I was bitter at the social sanctions my classmates had collared me with, I wanted to reconcile the problems I had with them. Every fall, the university would run an intramural flag football league. Some of the guys in my class, including Alan and Mason, had played during our first year. Second year, I came out to play with them. That was no fun at all. What a bunch of ball hogs! I would come out and run around with them for an hour or so and seldom get the ball at all. It isn't like I wanted it every time, but it would have been nice to get it actually thrown to me once in a while. The funny thing is, I played football in high school and none of the other guys had done the same except Alan. What's more, I was a pretty decent athlete, and I was getting treated like a scrub. Most of the other people on the team would get the ball a bit, but if the quarterback actually chose to throw the thing my way, it would usually be a bad throw that I couldn't get to. Then I wouldn't see the ball again for the whole night. I started to get the feeling that my teammates were conspiring against me, but instead of quitting, I decided to play that much harder—especially on defense. I needed the exercise anyhow, and I wasn't going to back down from those guys. I even pulled my hamstring pretty badly one night in the freezing cold, but I just tried to rehab it. I kept coming out.

One evening, as we played, Mason threw all the work we had done to reconcile our differences out the window. He was returning a kickoff after the other team scored, and I was trying to "block" for him. (Blocking in flag football entails trying to stand in front of the defensive players with your hands down at your sides.) As Mason came up the left sideline, I ran back towards him. My intention was for him to pick a path and go around me, either to the right or the left. Instead of doing that, he decided I was hindering his efforts and yelled at me to "Get out of the way!" "What a jerk!" I thought. After the play was over, I calmly walked over to him and asked him not to yell at his teammates. After all, the game wasn't that important. He looked at me with disdain and said that he couldn't promise that he wouldn't do it again. If I was ever going to hit him, it was right then and there. I suppose he's lucky, because I didn't. I just swallowed my anger and kept playing. However, the days of Mason and I getting along were drawing to a rather rapid end.

During the summer, Steve, a friend of mine from home, had moved to the area. He had gotten a job with a company located in one of the surrounding cities and we started to hang out quite a bit. The two of us had moved out of our parents' houses when we were eighteen and gotten an apartment together. We lived together a couple of times after that as well, including right before I left for dental school. When Steve got to Veiltown, we also began to spend time with another guy named Errol. He was the brother of our former roommate Blake, and he had moved to the area around five years earlier. Steve had become friends with him, and I had met him a few times before. Errol was a good guy, and we got along well. It helped a good bit to have a couple of friends to spend time with.

One Saturday night, I was driving home from hanging out with Steve and Errol at Steve's place. It was about three o'clock AM. I was entering an intersection about five minutes from my house when I looked to my right and realized that there was a car coming fast. It didn't take me long to figure out that it had absolutely no chance of not hitting me. Reflexively, my right foot came off the gas and went for the brake, but it was far too late. The driver plowed his late eighties Honda right into my front right fender. My driver's airbag popped out, and smoke from the propellant filled the cabin of the car. As I spun around in circles for what seemed like minutes, my internal dialogue went something like this: "Am I dying? I can't tell yet." When the spinning stopped, the car was angled towards the light that I was to be driving under, and it turned from green to yellow to red in front of me. I checked myself quickly to find that I was seemingly intact. My heart was racing, and I could feel that my right leg had slammed into something really hard, because it hurt quite a bit. I was alive though. I unbuckled my safety belt and stepped out onto the ground, placing weight on my injured leg to test and see if it was broken. I could tell that it wasn't, and I walked over to the other guy's car to see if he was injured. His car had spun and slammed rear-first into a light pole on the corner. I approached him to find he was conscious, just sitting in his seat. He looked a little too relaxed for someone who had just almost killed himself, and I suspected he had been using alcohol or some other mind-altering substance. When I asked if he was alright, his very slow reply was, "Why did you do that?" I was confused as to what he was asking, so I asked him what he meant. He asked, "Why did you run the red light?" I stood there stunned for a second, looking at him incredulously. Then I replied, "Nah man. YOU ran the red light." At that point, I didn't give a damn about his condition. Imagine that! He almost killed us both and then had the nerve to blame it on me! What the?!

As I walked back to my car, a young lady who had pulled over came walking towards me and asked me if I was okay. I said I was. She said she had just called the police. Then she looked at me for a second and accused me of being on drugs (as if I wasn't pissed enough)! "What are you talking about?" I asked. She said she was a doctor and that my pupils were completely dilated; they shouldn't be like that. I looked at her, trying not to spontaneously combust; then I took a deep breath and said, "Well Doctor, you must have been at the top of your class. Have you ever heard of adrenaline? Do you know what it does?" She just mouthed off something stupid (or at least I assumed it was stupid because of the previous things she had said). Then she walked back to her car and drove off. Unbelievable… I walked over to the service station on the corner and called Mara to let her know what had happened, then I came back and waited for the police.

As I waited, I examined my leg. It hurt more with each passing second, and it had started to swell. It had impacted the center console of the car about three inches above the ankle. The beginnings of a bruise went all the way through the muscle to the other side of my leg. I considered myself lucky to not have broken it as the force of the impact was pretty high. I also thanked the heavens for the fact that I hadn't eaten the airbag. Luckily, the angle of impact had thrown my torso sideways towards the car that hit me and had moved me out of the way of the inflating airbag. I was relieved because I knew that an airbag could do a number on your face, and I hated it when I had injuries on my head and face. I was happy to have escaped relatively unscathed. My leg seemed to be bruised pretty badly, but I doubted it was serious. It definitely could have been worse.

The police and an ambulance came a few minutes later. The paramedics asked me some questions and went to tend to the other guy, who was still just sitting in his car. Some officers talked with me about what had happened and such, and some others talked to the other guy. As it turned out, he did not have a license or insurance or registration for the car. I asked them if he was drunk or high, and they said he wasn't drunk, but they couldn't test for drugs right on the scene. I was a little upset, to put it mildly. I asked them if they were going to arrest him for all of the other illegal stuff. They said they wished they could, but they weren't allowed to. Go figure. Of course the police couldn't do their jobs within the bounds of our ridiculous legal system. Why would I think that they could? They could see my frustration and were very sympathetic, but their hands were tied. I got dropped off in front of the house by one of the officers at about four-thirty AM, and I went inside.

Mara was worried, but I assured her that I was alright. I gave her all the details, and we got to bed around six in the morning. I awoke maybe an hour later in a tremendous amount of pain. It turns out that when you have a muscle contusion, the pain is limited when the muscle is being used. When the muscle stands still for an extended period though, it tightens up. This isn't a problem until you try to move it again; when you do, watch out! I guess I moved my leg a bit while I was sleeping. When I came to, it hurt so bad that I almost vomited. I had to go run hot water in the bathtub and sit in it for fifteen minutes to decrease the pain enough to go back to sleep. I woke up five hours later to the same pain, and I had to soak the leg again. I was still tired and wanted to go back to sleep, but I didn't want to go through that torture again, so I just stayed up. After I soaked and moved around a bit, my purple, yellow, blue, and red leg felt a lot better.

Mara and I were stuck without a car for a couple of days. We both had cars, but had decided that we would only need one between the two of us in Veiltown. We left mine with my parents. (It was Mara's car that I had been driving when the accident happened.) My father drove my car in from Nampa as soon as he could, then he flew back home. My old Honda Civic hatchback was in pretty bad shape, as far as how it ran, so I took it in and got it checked out. It needed about eight hundred dollars worth of work. That wasn't a big deal because, between our combined student loans, Mara and I could easily afford to pay it. The eighteen hundred dollars we got for living expenses each month were more than enough for everything we needed, and even for the occasional emergency. As I have said before, the guy who caused the accident didn't have insurance, and Mara and I only had the bare minimum. As a result of that, we got a whopping fifty bucks when we sold the car to a salvage yard. We would have had to take the guy who hit me to small claims court to get what the car was worth, and with my schedule the way it was, I just couldn't go to all the trouble of missing school and getting behind on my lab work and assignments. Besides, it was a pretty sure bet that he wouldn't pay even if he was mandated to by the court. We had little choice but to eat the cost of the car. At least we had mine. Yes, it looked pretty torn down (my father had crashed his tractor into the front left fender and light, and it badly needed a paint job), but it ran well after the repairs were done. The alternative of taking the bus every day made us very thankful to have a spare.

Fortunately for me, I wasn't able to play flag football with my classmates anymore. I was tired of them anyhow. I wouldn't have quit, but I was glad to not have to go out and run around with them, never getting the ball, while freezing my ass off. Unfortunately, contrary to my intentions, I had not mended any fences by coming out and playing with them. I felt bitter at all of them for not allowing me to be a contributing part of the team, but it also made me lonelier. I guessed I would have to find another way to work my way into their graces.

It took quite a while for my leg to heal. Every morning for a week after the accident, I woke up in intense pain. It hurt so much that I began to dread sleeping. I knew that when I awoke, I was going to feel like someone had just hit me in the leg with a baseball bat. However, I was already spent from just going to school, even though I had adopted a policy of doing only minimal homework. No matter how distraught I was about sleeping, eventually, sheer exhaustion would overtake me. The first time I woke up and didn't have to hop to the bathroom to soak my leg, I was elated. Besides the morning pain, the injury didn't hamper my everyday life too much. I couldn't work my legs at the gym for a few weeks, but I kept up on my upper body. As my troubles went, my leg injury was a minor inconvenience.

10

The Battle for Sanity

The year progressed, and I got more and more tired of school. Second year at my school was the year in which the students learned to use drills and other dental instruments by practicing doing fillings, crowns, and other such restorations (on fake plastic teeth and real extracted teeth). We spent most of our time in the simulation lab, and we had so many projects and tests that missing even a day was difficult to recover from, at least for most of us. About halfway through the first quarter of the year, I decided that sleeping in lectures was an inefficient use of my time. I was neither learning nor getting any quality sleep, so I started to skip the classes that didn't take roll. That was most of them. I would sleep in an extra hour and come to school for lab. Most of the teachers had no clue that I wasn't there, and I would read over the material that they covered that day when I got around to it. Not a big deal. Inevitably, there was one lecture where the professor became wise to my routine. Of course, it isn't as though I tried to hide it from her—I more just threw it in her face.

The course was Oral Pathology (diseases of the mouth). In my opinion, the professor who taught the class (although extremely knowledgeable) was ridiculously haphazard and disorganized as a teacher. We met twice a week, and each time, we had to turn in homework that had been assigned to us previously. On one of the days, we had to take a little quiz as well. I had to at least be there to turn in the homework and take the quiz, but there was no way I was going to stay for her rat's nest of a lecture. There were naps to take! The classroom that the course was held in had stadium seating; and the entrance, to my chagrin, was at the bottom of the room. That meant I would have to pass the professor to get out. At first, I was hesitant to just leave right in front of her; but on a day when I was particularly tired, I thought, "Screw it" and walked out of the room (carrying my backpack and wearing my jacket). It was clear that I wasn't going to the bathroom. There was a lounge on the fourth floor of the building, and I went and slept there on the one couch that was long enough to accommodate my six feet two inch frame. I snoozed until I had to go to lab. The professor may have thought that I had something important to attend to that day—until I left again the next time class met. I came down to turn in my quiz with everyone else, placed it in the stack, and headed for the exit. I could feel the professor's eyes piercing into my back as I strolled casually towards the door. The next time class met, she watched me attentively as I walked into the room, placed my assignment in the stack, smiled at her sheepishly, and headed for the lounge. I can't deny, the look on her face was classic. She must have thought that I had some nerve. I didn't care though. She didn't have an attendance policy, so technically, I couldn't get in trouble (unless she retroactively altered her syllabus); and I wasn't going to waste my time in a class that I would have had a hard time paying attention in even if I wasn't sleep deprived—especially given my state of mind.

When we took the midterm, I got an eighty-five percent (which was pretty high comparatively). I simply crammed the night before. Everything she went over in class was in the course packet she had distributed, so it wasn't like I was missing out on information by skipping the professor's lectures. Even so, she had grown indignant at my policy of non-attendance, and she talked to the dean of student affairs about me. Unbeknownst to her, I had become quite friendly with him. Dr. Kreidler was a kind fellow, and he really liked to go to bat for the students. Unlike most of the faculty, he genuinely seemed to understand how unreasonable the curriculum was. I had spent quite a few hours with him, venting about how mistreated I felt as a student at the school. Dr. Kreidler always had an ear for me, and I appreciated it. When my Oral Pathology professor brought up my lack of attendance at her lectures, he called me into his office to talk. I told him exactly where I was at and how I felt about her teaching style. If I was going to sleep, I figured I should do it in a place where it would actually be restful. And make no mistake about it, I WAS going to sleep, either in her class or outside of it. I felt the professor's lecture was disorganized and difficult (if not impossible) for me to learn from. Besides, I had done just fine on my first test without attending her lectures or paying attention to her when I had. It wasn't like I wasn't learning anything. I could tell that he understood, and he told me he would take care of it. We talked about it a couple of days later, and he informed me that he had told my professor to "just leave him alone." I couldn't help but smile at that.

After the dean refused to do anything about my attendance, my professor decided to talk to me directly. She called me into her office, and we chatted for a good forty-five minutes. I wasn't disrespectful at all, but I told her directly how I felt about her lecture style. I also explained how much I disliked the program at our school and how I was terribly sleep deprived. With all of those things in the mix, I didn't feel that attending her lecture would serve any purpose; I more felt that doing so would be a detriment. She still wanted me to come to her lectures. She even tried to convince me to by telling me I had the lowest score in the entire class on the slide identification portion of the test we had just taken. (I knew it wasn't true.) I told her that if I came, there was no way I would be able to stay awake; I would just be sleeping in her class. Was that somehow less disrespectful than not coming? As I have said before, there was no attendance policy in her course. That meant she couldn't punish me for not coming, as long as I turned in my assignments and took her quizzes. Being a fair-minded person, she had to concede (albeit grudgingly). It was a pretty cool feeling to win a conflict with a teacher at that school, considering how they routinely bent us over. I was fortunate that she was the only professor who knew that I wasn't attending lecture that year though. I'm not sure that any of the others would have given in.

Eventually, after watching Mason continue to do the same things second year that he had done during first year, I lost patience with him. The incident during flag football had returned me to disliking him, and it had only been a matter of time before his disrespect for other people pushed me over the edge. I told our mutual friend to relay to Mason that if he so much as talked to me again, I was going to verbally rip him to shreds; and I wouldn't care who was around when it happened. Once the message was delivered, Mason obliged by not speaking to me again. It was a nice reprieve, although I still couldn't help but be infuriated by just the sound of his voice. Somehow, I finished the year without killing him, even though we spent most of our time only two seats apart.

My effort level had progressively died off during the year. I was skating by on pure god-given ability by the end. At the beginning of the year, I would still "study" at least a bit. I wasn't going to class or paying attention if I was there, but I would put in a few good hours before tests and such. By the time third quarter of second year came, I would quickly look over the materials for each test or quiz the night before. My effort level couldn't have really been less. All I cared about by that time was general concepts, and I refused to memorize anything. If I had to memorize it, I just didn't learn it. I got some really low grades (for me), but I passed all of my classes. My overall G.P.A. dropped a bit, but leveled out around three point five. That was still not bad, so I didn't have any reason to try harder, as far as I was concerned.

Despite the fact that I didn't really work that much outside of my time at school, both mentally and emotionally, things got harder and harder for me. When I was at school, I was a different person. I was really worried about the way people viewed me, so I put on an act. I never had any questions in any of the classes that I came to. Then again, I guess it's hard to ask questions when you are sleeping. I tried especially hard to be nice and non-offensive to anyone I had dealings with, save for Mason. I wanted to offend him. But since we didn't speak to each other anymore, the chances of any unpleasantness between us were slim to none. Even though I tried to mend fences with my other classmates, I felt more and more alone. I still heard rumors about things people had said about me, and some people in the class that I had no problem with at all gave off the nastiest vibes when I interacted with them. (A lot of them were the people who liked Mason. Maybe that had something to do with it.) One day, someone in the class who I actually got along with told me that I was really different than I had been during first year, and I could tell by his tone that he thought it was a good thing. It really made me angry—but sad at the same time. I hadn't really changed! It was just a façade. I guessed I had to be fake for people to accept me in that place. It figured. I had lost out on joining any social circles during first year because I studied so much. Then I stopped studying with Brendan and Eddie after the year ended, and that eliminated the vast majority of my social interaction within the school. By that point, most people had no inclination to include me in anything. My window of opportunity had closed. The few people that I did get along with were too busy outside of school or lived too far away to get together with often. (Once in a while, I would hang with Brendan.) I had Errol and Steve though, and I spent most of my free time with them. It helped, but even that would eventually go sour.

11

Weary Hearts

Throughout second year, my relationship with Mara got worse and worse. Somewhere along the way, we just stopped communicating. I think it stemmed from our constitutional personality differences. When it comes to emotions, I'm pretty expulsive. If I'm happy, you'll know it. If I'm sad, you'll know it. If I'm angry, you'll know it. I generally don't hold things in. Mara, on the other hand, is more the type to bottle up her emotions. She isn't good at venting and has a tendency to hold negative emotions in and brood over them. A lot of times, when I felt like talking, she wouldn't respond to anything I said. I took it as an insult, and because I was feeling so rotten inside, I started to lash out at her. I was supposed to be able to find solace in her, but gradually, day-by-day, she got further and further away. It probably didn't help that I got angry when she stonewalled me. At any rate, eventually, rather than getting upset and trying to force her to give me what I needed, I started ignoring her too. I remember coming home and being unhappy to see her. How did that happen? She used to be the best thing in my world; all my future plans revolved around her. We were going to build a life together. Yet by the time the end of second year came around, I was fighting with myself daily, trying to keep from ending it all. There were still things that were worth fighting for, I realized later; but at the time, I couldn't see anything but how angry she made me by pushing me away. I began pushing back, and the gap between us grew larger and larger. We did have love, and I should have been able to do what I had to do to protect it. When she started pushing me away, instead of pushing back, I should have pulled her close. But I didn't. Soon enough, I just couldn't hang on to the thin thread that tethered us together. So I let go…

We got into an argument about nothing one night in April, right around the time of both of our birthdays. Same old shit: Mara being cold and me blowing up about it. After a few minutes of arguing, I just blurted it out: "I'm through with you. We're finished." I almost couldn't believe I said it. Just as she had done when I told her that Jake had died, Mara instantaneously burst into tears. It was extremely difficult for me to watch because, even though I was furious with her for shutting me out of her life, I still cared about her deeply. She was the first woman I had ever loved... She had loved me for almost eight years—for the better parts of my nature and in spite of the worse parts. It isn't easy to end that sort of thing, no matter how set on it you might be; you can't help but remember all of the things that made you stay so long in the first place. My mind was made up though, so I could only spend the rest of the night talking with her and trying to explain why I had to do what I was doing. It wasn't like I was the only one who was unhappy in our relationship. She was hurting too, and it was obvious. Through the tears that ran down her face and the pent up emotions that were justifiably releasing from the vault she kept locked inside of her, she had the wherewithal to say this to me: "What about the plans we made? We spent so much time building this, and I don't know how I can be okay with it not happening now." I guess she wanted me to cry too… But even though my eyes glossed over, and deep inside, a part of me felt the same, I knew that it was better for both of us that we go our separate ways. We had done too much damage to ever go back. We went to sleep later on, both with heavy hearts, next to each other in our bed.

12

Reminders

After Mara and I broke up, we had an inescapable issue to deal with: we still lived together. Our two-year lease wasn't going to expire for a few more months at that point, so we were stuck being a broken up couple who cohabited. We still even slept in the same bed. To a lot of people, that might sound like a bad thing. In truth, it turned out to be one of the best things that could have happened (given the circumstances). As I have said before, I was really angry at Mara when I finally ended our relationship. I felt like it was almost entirely her fault that we couldn't stay together. In my mind, she had driven me away by being closed up and generally negative. If I had any part in it, I couldn't see it. I had merely reacted justifiably to her coldness. I still cared for her, but in my anger, I actually believed that I disliked her to some extent. Living with her for that few months more really showed me some things that I needed to see. Without a romantic relationship to get in the way, we started to communicate again and to actually talk about things like we used to. After a little bit of time, I realized that I wasn't angry with her anymore and that I still loved her deeply, if only as a friend. I remembered the person she was inside once more, and that person was still kind and generous and intelligent and worth keeping in my life. We even had a bit of fun together making light of the people each other chose to date. When I think of how most people break up and just continue on hating each other, I thank the heavens that we were able to find a friendship in the ruins of our love.

13

The Single Life

By the end of my time with Mara, I was certain that romantic "love" was just a fabricated notion. I was sure that I had given my best to our relationship, and it had ultimately rewarded me only with heartache. If two smart, caring, devoted people like Mara and I couldn't keep it together, how could anyone else (unless they were just fooling themselves)? Everyone that I knew whose parents were still together said the same thing: "I don't think they love each other anymore." It seemed that romantic love was actually just acceptance—the inability to change an old habit. For whatever reason, it appeared that all the excitement and passion were destined to die in every relationship. After that, only familiarity and friendship would remain (if that). Due to that perception, I was certain that I would never have a girlfriend again. My intention was to only have casual relationships and stay uncommitted.

One good thing about being newly single (which actually turned out to be a very bad thing in the long run) was that I didn't have to be financially responsible anymore. Mara and I had pooled our money while we were together, and I had made sure to keep my spending to prudent levels during that time.

When I broke up with her, all my inhibitions about spending went straight into the nearest dumpster. I had always liked buying things, and I took the credit that I had built up over the past few years and promptly ruined it. First, I bought eight hundred dollars worth of clothing. Then, I decided that I just couldn't be out there dating with my car in the condition it was in. I had to fix it up. I put eight thousand dollars into bodywork, a new paint job, new wheels and tires, and an alarm and GPS tracking system to protect against theft. The car looked pretty good by the time I was done with it, and I figured that I would easily be able to pay off the credit cards once I graduated and started working. And anyhow, I was willing to pay some interest to have a little bit of enjoyment in the present, especially after all of the crap I had gone through during my first two years of school. I guess I don't regret the decision now, but sometimes I come really close. At any rate, I wasn't newly single and cruising around in a hoopty.

It really did feel like I had been single for quite a while, due to the lack of affection in my relationship with Mara. It had been a long time since I dated, and I was excited to get back out there and see how I would do. I knew I was a bit rusty at "the game," so to start off, I decided to try out a popular online dating site. I went on a few dates with some girls I met there, and it wasn't long before I met one that I was interested in. Kristina was a tall, blonde college basketball player for one of the local universities. She was a bit shy, but also intelligent, competitive, and a lot of fun to be around. We dated for about three months. By the end of that period (after spending a good deal of time with her) I was willing to get into a committed relationship. (I guess I didn't know myself as well as I had originally thought.) It was pretty quick for me to want a girlfriend again, but I did. I enjoyed being around Kristina, so why did I need to date other girls? Nonetheless, in the way of my desire to be her boyfriend was the fact that she was nursing a pretty bad wound from a guy she had been in love with before we met. He had cheated on her multiple times with multiple different women. She had tried to forgive him and trust him again, but it was to no avail. Eventually, she left him, but her heart was broken from the whole ordeal. She just didn't have it in her to get into a relationship with me, regardless of how I attempted to convince her. When she broke off our romantic endeavors, I didn't get upset or cry or pout or anything like that though. I just told her that I didn't want to end it, but if that was her decision, I would have to accept it. Humorously, at least from my point of view, she told me that the way I handled the situation was a "turn-on." All I could think was, "Silly girl. You don't know what you want." After that, we kept in contact and grew to be close friends, and I'm happy for that.

After Kristina, the real dating adventure began. I cancelled my membership to the dating website, arrogantly deciding that only defective people used dating websites and that only losers with no guts met women that way. As far as I was concerned, in order to be a real man, a guy needed to be brave enough to go talk to women. Courage was the order of the day, and I was going to figure out how to get dates from women without the help of the World Wide Web. I hadn't "macked" in nearly eight years, so hitting on woman proved to be somewhat nerve-wracking at first. I had to get really psyched up to do it. I guess it was hard for me because I imagined that any woman I wanted to talk to might be a wonderful, intelligent, motivated, kind one who I could have something lasting with. (I never saw women as conquests.) Luckily, after a few clumsy attempts that ended in failure, I started to come off much more confidently. I was bold; that was for sure. If I saw a woman that I wanted to hit on, I would do it, no matter where I happened to be at the moment. I hit on women in grocery stores, at the gym, in coffee shops, at the mall, in restaurants, at the park. I even did it at the library. My approach was simple and to the point: I would say hi, introduce myself, tell the woman I thought she was beautiful, stunning, attractive, gorgeous, etc, and then I would ask if she was single. If she was, I would ask her if she would let me take her out some time. To my satisfaction, I got quite a few phone numbers and e-mail addresses. My confidence soared. At the very least, I usually got a genuine smile and a "thank you" if the girl was already taken. Some of the women may have lied, I know, but not once did any of them ever say that they were single but not interested. I think my approach was so unorthodox and brave that many of them were impressed with the level of forwardness it took. (I mean really, who hits on a woman at IKEA?)

I once heard about an article that was published in a well known nationally circulated magazine where a survey of men had singled out Veiltown as the worst dating city in the nation. I don't know if the article actually exists, and at the time I had never really dated anywhere else, but I have to say that I can't imagine dating being any more difficult than it was for me in that city. It just seemed to me that the women there were very closed-minded and judgmental. I ran into all sorts of problems. Often, I would call a woman whose number I had gotten, and she would never answer her phone or return my call. I wondered why the women who did that sort of thing had even given me their numbers to begin with. I would have much preferred an honest "no" to the waiting and wondering inflicted on me by the blow-offs I received. If I did actually communicate with a woman after initial contact, other problems seemed to arise rapidly. For my part, I was determined to give any woman I went out with a chance to show me who she was. I definitely wasn't arrogant enough to think that I could know the depths of someone after a few short conversations or one date. People are so much more than any one experience with them usually makes clear. It seemed that the women I dated didn't see it that way. I think a lot of them came into dates with me having already made up their minds that we didn't have any sort of future together. In the cases where my dates were actually open to the idea that we might be able to continue forward, my personality put a quick stop to that. Most of the women I met there were quite reserved. They didn't have a whole lot to say about anything, at least not to a guy they had just met. On the other hand, I have this habit of filling silence with words. I don't have to be asked a question to talk, and if I am asked a question, I will usually answer it and then some. It's just the way my mind works. It starts going off in a hundred different directions once a topic of discussion is brought up. To those women, I guess I seemed like the most abrasive, overly opinionated loudmouth, or like some attention-starved child, jumping up and down yelling, "Look at me! Look at what I can do!"

Another problem I had dating in Veiltown was that many of the women I approached were very certain that I was a "player." (Some of them even came right out and told me so.) While I was flattered that they thought I was attractive enough to be a womanizer, the perception still frustrated me. I wondered why presenting myself the way I did automatically made me appear dishonest and selfish. Being a sensitive person, it hurt quite a bit to find out that the nice girls I tried to talk to were afraid of getting involved with me because they were certain that I would mislead them and abuse their trust. What did they want from me? Was I supposed to wear crappy clothing and stop lifting weights so I would look "safer?"

It is a bad habit of human beings indeed to make snap judgments about others based on first impressions and situational reactions. If you think it isn't true, think about a time when you saw a customer yelling at a clerk at the store. You didn't know what happened to that person earlier in the day or the week. Maybe one of his loved ones had died. Maybe he just got laid off at work. And you didn't know what kind of person he really was or what kind of values he held close to his heart. All you saw was how rude he was to the clerk—how he flew off the handle. Did you stand there and think about the possibilities, or did you judge him because he was doing something that was socially unacceptable? Don't get me wrong—I'm not criticizing you if you did. I have done the same many times, and I even still do so reflexively. But think about all the times you have messed up and made yourself look bad. Would it be fair for someone to think they could peg you and everything you are based off of one moment of weakness? I didn't want to think that way anymore, and at any rate, I have great friends who I routinely disagree with in both thought and action; so even if a woman made a less than spectacular impression on me, I still fully intended to get to know her better and to try to really understand her. I guess it was just asking too much for those women to do the same, especially with possible romantic intentions involved. My personality, on the surface, was not what the women in that city thought was one that would belong to a good man. I guess I gave off the vibe that I was full of myself and selfish, when nothing could have been further from the truth. Nonetheless, even after a few bad experiences, I figured it was just a matter of persistence until I found someone I could really click with. My experience with Kristina had opened my eyes to the fact that I was still the same, and without a doubt, I wanted to love again. This time though, I wanted it to last.

14

Dislike as a Habit

At the end of the second year of dental school, we had to take the first part of a two-part written national board exam for licensure. It was a four-part test with one hundred questions in each section, and it covered four basic subjects that we had gone over mostly during first year. My school had formerly made its students take the test after first year, but they had changed it recently so that more of the subjects on the test could be covered before the examination. I guess it had improved test scores because even though postponing the test gave the students time to forget a large portion of the things they learned, they made up for it by studying hard enough to re-solidify the knowledge. The school gave us one full week off of classes and also a week of half-days so that we could study right before the test. The classes before us had only gotten a week of half-days, but the faculty had mercifully made a change, effective that year, to take the pressure off of us. It was a nice gesture for sure, but I didn't care enough about school by that point to appreciate it fully. I did think about studying, and I debated doing so up until our time off started; but when the time came, I just couldn't bring myself to put any effort into it. I came to the decision that I wouldn't study. For one, the test would be over things that would not help me be a better dentist. The subjects were: anatomic sciences, biochemistry/physiology, microbiology/pathology, and dental anatomy/occlusion. To the outside observer, it might appear that the subject "dental anatomy/occlusion" would have some relevance to dentistry, but the kind of questions asked to test us on this subject had nothing to do with actually being a dentist. They were more like dental trivia. "Generally, which is the tallest cusp on the maxillary first molar?" I can't think of one clinical situation where that sort of knowledge could even be considered remotely useful. If you are a dentist and can, please do contact me. The other three subjects were too general to be useful. I understand why we had to learn them, but I couldn't see why we would be tested on such things. When our time off came, I just hung out. I didn't do anything academic for the entire week off, and it felt pretty refreshing. I just focused on dating and exercise. In fact, I met Kristina during that week.

My reasoning for not studying went something like this: the subjects were extraneous, and I would memorize the information only to forget it soon afterwards; I would also never use any of that information in dentistry (except maybe a small piece of the head and neck portion of anatomical sciences, and I knew the parts of that subject that I would be using pretty well by that point). All else aside, I was fully aware that there was a possibility that I would fail; but if I did, I would simply put in a little effort, study, take the test again, and pass. It was a calculated risk, and I was not at all unconfident in my ability to do what I needed to do, if and when I needed to do it. I just didn't see the utility in spending my time studying for something so worthless if there was any chance I could pass without doing so. Like a fool, I let it get out that I wasn't going to study for the exam, but I did explain my exact reasoning to anyone I talked to about it. Naturally, my well-explained and logical reasons were soon twisted into: "Darren thinks he's so smart that he doesn't have to study for the board exam." ??? When did I say that? Didn't I say that I knew I might fail, but wasn't afraid to risk it if there was a chance I could pass without studying? I did say those things, but people just wanted a reason to hate me, especially considering my past troubles. Again, despite my efforts to fight it, the perceptions of others were less than favorable about me. I was a red speck in a pond of gray, and that made most of my schoolmates mad. No matter what I did or how hard I tried to fit in with them, they had already made up their minds that I wasn't likable. Anything I did that was at all against the status quo would only bring me more disapproval.

When the scores came, I did in fact pass all four sections. Nevertheless, I did extremely poorly. Two of my scores were in the eighth percentile. That means that ninety-two percent of the people who took the test did better than me on that section. The rest of my class had done very well as a whole. Our class average was fifth best in the nation in fact. And you know what? I got a huge kick out of the fact that I could have done just as well as anyone but chose not to, therefore driving down our class's average significantly. I knew that quite a few people were bitter at me for the whole situation, and honestly, I was glad.

15

The Writing on the Wall

Around the beginning of my third year in school, I got a bit of a reprieve from my suffering. That came in the form of two people. One reentered my life, and another came into it for the first time. In the midst of my struggle to prove my own inner strength to myself, I was loath to understand just how important their presence was to me. I only knew that they helped ease my loneliness, if just temporarily.

DJ had been one of my closest friends since I was a senior in high school. We met during our junior year but didn't become friends until the beginning of twelfth grade. The funny thing about it was that we both started out with gross misperceptions of the other. He had mouthed off to one of my favorite teachers in the English course we had together as juniors, and I thought he was a slacker. Based on the way I dressed and the people I hung out with, he assumed that I was some cocky prick. DJ was a skater and I was "hip-hop." On the surface, we couldn't have been more different. However, when we started talking on a regular basis, we quickly became the best of friends. To both of our surprises, we were very similar in a lot of ways, but still just different enough to make things interesting. We barely left each other's sides for our entire senior year. If we had free time, we were hanging out. We remained close over the years that followed.

After high school, DJ had attended a very prestigious school in Southern California while I had stayed at home. After he graduated college, DJ went to Japan for four years, teaching English for three of them and then doing some consulting work for the fourth. Before we had graduated college, knowing full-well that life might take us far from each other in the future, we made an agreement that we would attend post-undergraduate programs in the same city. We had originally wanted to end up in Veiltown. Although there were points when it looked like it might not happen, DJ started the PhD program for economics at the university I attended for dental school in the fall of my third year there.

I was so excited the day I picked DJ up from the airport. I was looking forward to being able to just kick it with him like we used to in high school. Mara had moved out earlier in the month to a rental house nearer the university, while DJ and I were going to be living with Errol a bit further from school. I was to keep the dogs with me, and Mara and I would figure out permanent custody later on. I was on a five-week vacation between summer and fall quarter of school, and DJ and I were going to get everything set up in our new dwellings, then drive back home to see his mother and brother. The day after DJ flew in, we rented a huge diesel moving truck (because they didn't have anything smaller) and took everything left in the house to the new spot. I got the privilege of driving the massive piece of... machinery. It was an utter miracle that I didn't bash the hell out of someone's car on the way. That experience gave me a newfound respect for semi-truck drivers, without a doubt, but I know for sure that I was relieved to be rid of that thing when we turned it in late in the afternoon. A few days later, we got in my car and headed for home.

The trip was, for the most part, a lot of fun. I got to see my good friend Dustin, who had been living in Arkansas and was visiting his family at the time. I also got to see my friends Ansel, Mike, and Scott, who all still lived in town. Notwithstanding, one thing that happened during the trip really rattled me. One night, DJ, Mike, Ansel, Dustin, Ansel's girlfriend Wendy, myself, and another friend of Ansel's named Jonas went to a driving range to hit some golf balls. It turned out that the range was closed. On the way back to the cars, we were talking about racquetball. Ansel was saying how his friend Marty was the best racquetball player he had ever seen; he thought that Marty could take DJ. As it happens, DJ is ridiculously good at that game. Ansel is pretty good as well, but when he and DJ had played years earlier, DJ stomped him good. I was with my best friends, in my hometown, and I was feeling like I could be myself after a full year of restraining my personality in an attempt to fit in at my dental school. I guess I was just a bit too much myself for Ansel to take that night. When he said Marty could take DJ, I jumped at the chance to talk some trash. I told Ansel that he was dreaming and that I would take that bet any day. Ansel responded by saying that he himself couldn't even compete with Marty most of the time. I responded by reminding Ansel of how DJ had housed him when they played a few years ago. He replied by saying that he was sick that day. I laughed at that, and I told him I didn't remember it being that way at all. His response to that wasn't verbal, nor was it friendly. Ansel looked at me with a bit of a perturbed smile. Then he reached out and sort of shoved me with both hands. I thought he was joking around at first, but then his face became unmistakably angry, and before I knew what was going on, he picked me up by the shirt and slammed me ass-first into a car in the parking lot. I wasn't injured, but I was stunned and bewildered at what had just happened. I stood there looking at him, confused, hurt, and increasingly angrier with each passing second. I don't remember what I said exactly. It was probably something to the effect of: "What the hell is your problem?" Dustin, DJ, Mike, and Jonas had jumped to the ready as soon as Ansel slammed me into the car, and they were ready to stop anything else that was going to go down. It was a good thing too, because after a few seconds of jawing at Ansel while growing progressively more distraught, I decided that I was ready to take a beating. (That is exactly what I would have ended up with too, as Ansel was much bigger, stronger, and more aggressive than I happened to be.) I quickly moved forward to give Ansel a piece of my… fist, but DJ and Mike grabbed me and held me back the best they could as Jonas and Dustin got in front of Ansel and pushed him away from the area. He didn't resist and just backed up. I know that he didn't want to hurt me, even though I obviously couldn't say the same with regards to him at that moment. I managed to rip free of DJ and Mike once, but they quickly grabbed me again and locked me up until Ansel and I were sufficiently far apart. It took a minute, but after I calmed down, they let me go. Once my arms were free, I needed to do something with them, so I reached into my pockets and grabbed my keys, my wallet, and my change. Then I shouted out expletives as I fired all of them into the night sky like I was throwing Hail Mary passes at the end of the Super Bowl. My keys weren't on a standard key chain, so when they hit the ground they scattered in all directions. It took quite a while for us to find all of the important pieces of my belongings, such as my car key and my credit cards. Luckily for me, a wallet has a lot of wind drag. Keys, on the other hand, do not. I was surprised at how strong my arm was when we found most of my keys much further away than we had been looking. Then again, my throws had been adrenaline assisted.

After that, we all went bowling. ??? I went over to Ansel after we had been playing for a while and apologized for making him mad. I didn't mean to be insensitive. I was just talking trash like we always did. I really couldn't understand why what I said had set Ansel off so violently, but I felt remorseful for it. Ansel has never been as open with his feelings as I am, so he didn't explain much. Even so, he told me he was sorry and that everything was cool. Looking back, I can see now that Ansel was pretty stressed out too. (He had just finished his first year of dental school.) I wish I had figured that out before I shot my mouth off.

As a side note, on the way out of the bowling alley, this short, younger looking kid who was very intoxicated tried to pick a fight with Jonas. All my frustration and sadness had me about to burst, so I couldn't help myself from getting involved. The kid was just being a drunken idiot, and in retrospect, I wish I had left Jonas to handle it on his own. Regardless, I did step in and tell the kid to go away. He was too drunk or stupid or both to back down, and he stepped up into my face. I grabbed him by his throat with one hand and shoved him to the ground. He got up and came back, so I shoved him again. Then he went to get his "friends," which turned out to be an even smaller young man and what looked to be his grandfather. All of us had a good laugh at the looks on their faces when they walked up to our group. (Mike, the shortest member of our crew, stood five feet nine inches tall and carried a lot of bulky muscle on him.) We left quickly after the two of them guided the drunk kid away, as it was apparent that security would soon be coming. I was in the lead as we left, and Ansel and Wendy brought up the rear. Security caught up to them, and they explained what happened. That bought some time for me to get away. The guards wanted to talk to me because I had been in a physical confrontation, but I was already off the premises by the time they finished talking to Ansel and Wendy. What a silly little display I put on. It just went to show how torn apart I was inside.

I was glad that Ansel was okay with the whole thing, but my sense of self-worth took another huge hit because it happened. This was one of my best friends who had taken me wrongly. He knew me and knew me well. This was a man who I would have stood by through anything. I would have even laid down my life for him, if the situation arose where I needed to. I just didn't understand how he could have misread me so badly after all the years we had known each other and been such good friends. When I had visited earlier that year, I met a few of Ansel's classmates. Par for the course, a few of them had bad things to say about me once I left. I didn't do anything or say anything inappropriate or condescending to any of them, but that didn't keep them from judging me as arrogant after the small amount of surface interaction we had. Not surprisingly, as I remember it, all of those people were actually from out of town. One of them was even from Veiltown. Besides that, Ansel had expressed some disapproval at my decision not to study for the board examination. He seemed really disappointed in me and told me that I was too smart to be so flippant about something as important as that. After our scuffle, I started to think that he had lost a lot of respect for me because I had let him down by not studying, but also because the people he was spending so much time around didn't like me. It seemed their opinions of me were rubbing off on him. Sadly, it was evident that Ansel's perception of me had somehow become unfavorable too. It was then that it dawned on me for the first time that all the naysayers might even be at least partially right. It was a hard pill to swallow, and most of me resisted the idea that I was at all to blame for my troubles. Nonetheless, the seed had been planted, and with time it would grow.

16

Something to Get You Through

School started up shortly after we got back from our trip. Back to the grind. I was somewhat less than excited to go back, but that was my path. Contrastingly, DJ (having been out of school for four years) was looking forward to getting back into the world of academia. I remembered how I had once looked forward to dental school—it seemed an eternity ago. The two years I had yet to complete seemed like an eternity as well. To my dismay, I seemingly had no choice.

The place we had moved to was around fifteen miles from campus and was actually three small cities away from Veiltown. That fact cut into my sleep time because I had to get up much earlier just to get to school on schedule. I would drive my car down to Veiltown, sometimes hitting traffic and sometimes missing it. Then I would park at a park-and-ride (a place where you can park your car for free and take a bus) and hop on the bus to school. I did that for the next year. It cost me a bit of money for gas, but more than anything, it contributed to my fatigue. That made attending school even more of a challenge.

A few days after DJ and I arrived back in Veiltown, Kristina and I played basketball at her college's gym. We played some one-on-one, then we joined the five-on-five games on the center court. Maybe an hour before we left, I got tangled up with a guy I was defending and his knee rammed directly into my left calf. The blow smarted, but I was able to walk it off and continue playing. Afterwards, while Kristina was driving us back to her place, I was examining my injury and found that the spot of impact looked as though it had a balloon inside of it. "Great…" When I woke up the next morning, the excruciating pain that I had grown familiar with after my car accident had made a disheartening return, only it had switched legs. I went to the campus health center that day, and they gave me some crutches and a prescription for a painkiller (very similar to Ibuprofen, except stronger). The painkiller was supposed to help with the pain, obviously, but it was also supposed to prevent the formation of bone inside of the muscle. (The sort of injury I suffered could sometimes cause that kind of maladaptive healing.) I had to take the painkiller multiple times each day, and it really upset my stomach. For a while, I was limping around school on crutches, and waking up in the morning again became my worst nightmare for a week or so. All I could do was wince in pain as I hopped up the stairs and into the bathroom to soak.

As the school year started, one thing I WAS looking forward to was seeing if there were any attractive women in the new first-year class. I knew that a woman who was attending dental school was, on average, very intelligent. That was a big turn-on for me. My class was definitely full of great-looking, intelligent woman. By then, all of them were taken, but I was hoping that the new class might have a few worthwhile girls who were single. There did turn out to be some very attractive women in the new class. One in particular caught my eye immediately. Liz was a tall, curvy brunette with a swagger about her. We ended up talking a few times at the beginning of the year because we just happened to ride the same bus. I didn't think her face was that great, but I really enjoyed her personality and the way she carried herself. She did have a boyfriend, but I didn't find out for a while, so I tried to interact with her as much as possible.

Something to Get You Through

I wasn't one for extracurricular activities, but because I knew Liz would be there, I ended up making an appearance at the inaugural "Wax and Relax": a couple of hours set up for the first year students to get technique lessons on waxing. I helped out as much as I could, and I ended up meeting quite a few interesting people, but I was really there so I could talk to Liz. Encouragingly, I did get a chance to spend some time talking to her, but aside from that, something very important happened to me that night. It was so important that I honestly can't begin to guess who I would be right now if I hadn't been there. It is entirely possible that I might have met the friend I met that night later. Maybe our relationship would even be as deep and important as it has become, but I can't be sure. Whatever the case may be, I just know that the course of my life was changed for the better that night.

The first things we said to each other were very typical. He greeted me, shook my hand, and introduced himself. "Hi, I'm Darren." I smiled and told him that my name was Darren as well. I'll never forget what he said next; it was the cornerstone of what our friendship has developed into. "No way… You're going to have to change that. What do you think of Darryl?" I started to laugh immediately. I told him that I was pretty sure I had the name first, so he was going to have to change his. He said he betted that he was older than me, but to his dismay, he fell short by two years. Darren had a unique look about him. He was my height with bright blue eyes and curly, dark brown hair covered by a white bandana. He wore clothing that was decidedly hip-hop, and I knew right away that he wasn't from Veiltown. When I asked, I found out that he was from San Francisco. As it turned out, he was concurrently studying for a PhD along with his doctoral degree in dentistry. Darren also had a bachelor's degree and a master's degree from an extremely respected university. This was an intelligent guy. We spent quite a few minutes chatting while he made teeth out of wax with his Bunsen burner and metal instruments. The conversation wasn't just small talk though. He was open and honest, and I felt that I knew a fair amount about him and who he was when we parted that night. I had met few people like that since I

79

had been in Veiltown, and it was a welcome experience. We ended up exchanging numbers. It is not untrue to say that I had a good feeling about Darren right from the start.

When we first talked on the phone, true to form, I said something that was possibly too forward (at least for most people). I told Darren that I could see him and I becoming good friends. He didn't respond poorly to it though, so I didn't have any reason to think it might have been inappropriate. Subsequently, we began to hang out regularly. I enjoyed being around him because there was substance to him. He never wanted to turn off his brain. He was always down for deep discussions about issues of importance, or just intellectual conversations about inconsequential things. We had a great time because of that fact. I'm not saying that deep conversations were all we would spend our time on. For sure, we would go to the clubs and dance or throw a football or Frisbee around. Whenever we talked though, it was stimulating, and I appreciated that. On top of his huge intellect, Darren was easy-going, expressive, and unselfish. Having him and DJ around helped me pass the time and keep my mind off school. They provided a much-needed escape.

17

Clinic

Third year in dental school greatly tested my patience. In fact, it almost broke my patience. We basically jumped into the clinical life. On top of classes in the early morning, we started seeing patients on a regular basis, in multiple different clinics. We would often get out of class with just five or ten minutes to get to the clinic and set up all of our instruments to work. We also had to do basically everything by ourselves. I think there may be some schools that have a large supply of employees to help the students with the numerous odd tasks that make up so much of dentistry, but ours was not among them. We had to bag our instruments and transport them to sterilization, put barriers on the parts of our little assigned cubicles that would be exposed to flying saliva and blood, and spray and wipe down our counters and chairs. When we were actually doing dentistry on a real live patient, there were only a few assistants, so we had to do things that were really better performed by two people all by ourselves. Those things were annoying and time consuming, but bearable. What was nearly unbearable was the fact that we had to schedule our own patients in the restorative dentistry, periodontics (gum health), and prosthodontics (dentures) clinics. It just took so much time. The most infuriating part about it was the fact that attendance was a consideration in grading and the patients could be very unreliable. They would often cancel at the last possible minute or just not show up. After all the time we had to spend tracking them down and scheduling them, waiting an hour to find that a patient was not coming could really test one's fortitude (especially following a mad scramble to prepare after morning class). To compound all of that, missed sessions had to be made up later on.

I hated clinic quite a bit after a while, but at least I didn't have to listen to Mason talk anymore. Before we were assigned to our units in the clinic, I had gone to the people in charge of that task and asked them if I could be assigned to a different floor than Mason. (There were two clinics for restorative dentistry, and they were on separate floors.) I had to give a long explanation as to why I was requesting such a thing. Then I got to listen to the obligatory "You should be able to act professionally and get along with this person even though you don't like him" speech. Thankfully, the administration gave in and separated us. The best part of that was that they left me on the floor I would have been assigned to originally and moved Mason to the other floor. Even though that had not been my intention, I thought it was funny because it separated Mason from probably his best friend in our class Craig (who had sat between us in the simulation lab for the first two years). I didn't really care what floor I was on, but I did feel bad for the people that had to be around Mason on the other floor. At least the people in my area were already used to him. Oh well. It was too late to change anything.

One day during the second quarter of third year, I ended up right on the brink of making a life-altering decision. We got out of our morning lecture extremely late, and by the time I made it to the clinic from the other side of the building, it was five minutes past the time when my appointment was supposed to start. Luckily, I thought, my patient wasn't yet there. I scrambled to get my unit ready, and I got all my instruments from the sterilization room. By the time that was done, ten minutes had passed. My patient had not arrived, so I went to check my voicemail. Sure enough, my patient had called at three thirty in the daggone morning to tell me she wouldn't be coming. I felt absolutely abused. Every single thing about that experience made me irate: the inconsideration the professor showed by holding us over when he knew we had somewhere important to be; the huge hurry to get everything ready so the patient wouldn't have to be inconvenienced; and the all-too-frequent last second cancellation that I didn't have time to figure out before I rushed to set everything up. I was so damn tired of being treated that way, and I was done accepting it. I turned my unused instruments back in to sterilization and went directly to Dr. Kreidler's office. I told him I was through; I couldn't take the abuse anymore. He listened, as he always did, and told me I should think about it. He was right, but in my rage, I couldn't imagine changing my mind. I told him I would mull it over, but as far as I was concerned, there was nothing to think about. I didn't have anything scheduled for the afternoon, so that saved me the trouble of having to cancel it. I got on the bus and took it to the park-and-ride where my car was parked. Then I drove home. On the way, I called DJ. He didn't pick up, so I left him a message telling him that I was through with dental school. He called back a few minutes before I got home. I had once told him that if I ever tried to drop out of dental school, I wanted him to stop me, no matter what he had to do. He was quick to remind me of that fact, but I was still too angry to listen. DJ reasoned with me the best he could, but I refused to take it into consideration. Just as I had done with Dr. Kreidler, I told DJ I would think about what he said. Once again, I was sure I wasn't going to change my mind. I was home by the time we finished talking, and I got promptly into my bed and fell right to sleep.

When I awoke, I knew that my plan to drop out of dental school was merely wishful thinking. Over the last few months, I had considered a number of other career paths that I would need to get more education to pursue. I checked with the admissions office of the university to see if I could register for undergraduate classes under my current standing as a professional student, but they informed me that I would not be able to do so and would have to apply for admission just like everyone else. The next admission cycle was pretty far away, and I knew very well that I didn't have the patience to work some Joe job until I got back into undergraduate school. Waiting tables for what effectively amounted to "peanuts" was even more repulsive of a notion than continuing the abuse of dental school. I had devised a plan to finish dental school and work full-time as a dentist until I could get my debts under control. Once I had a handle on my finances, I could cut back to two or three days a week and go to school for something else—or just dabble in things so I could find something I enjoyed more than dentistry. Not finishing dental school wouldn't be very conducive to that goal. Besides that, I already owed the government over one hundred thousand dollars in student loans, and paying that off seemed a very distant event if I were to abandon dentistry altogether. I could have dropped out at that point, but honestly, the financial burden I was carrying was a bit overwhelming and also somewhat frightening. I had to resign myself to the fact that, even if I was only a dentist for a short time, barring an act of God, I was going to finish dental school.

18

Urgency

After that, the rest of my actual school time was pretty uniform. I would skip the lectures that I could, attend the ones I couldn't skip, and show up for clinic. I forced myself to ignore the hassles and mistreatment and, I decided to believe that I would get all of my requirements done in time, even in the face of setbacks and wasted days. After my near withdrawal from school, I had to choose not to worry about those things just to maintain some version of sanity. It wasn't too hard though, because in truth, none of those trifles mattered to me when I compared them to my social troubles. More and more, I felt like a fraud when I was at school as I tiptoed around, trying to keep everyone happy by squelching my personality. I wanted so desperately to be accepted, but I loathed that I had to put on an act to win my classmates' approval. I was conflicted and confused, and my heart cried out for shelter.

There were two women at the school that I made really bad mistakes with during third year. One was my age and had been separated from her husband for almost a year. Her name was Kara and she was in the class ahead of mine. I developed a bit of a crush on her after getting to know her some in clinic, but I was sensitive to her situation, and I didn't want to put any pressure on her by trying to ask her out. I did try to feel out the situation by asking a friend of hers if she thought there was any chance that Kara might want to date me. Kara's friend said that she was not looking to date anyone at the moment. Even so, I wanted to get to know her better and maybe make a friend, even if it never led to anything more. I felt like I could at least be someone she could trust and confide in. We exchanged e-mail addresses, and I tried to correspond with her over e-mail a bit after she graduated. Frustratingly, she really didn't make much of an attempt to talk with me. In my loneliness, I got dejected. After not hearing from her for almost three months (right around the end of my the summer session of my third year), I wrote her an e-mail and told her that she was hurting my feelings. Obviously, it was not my place to put that on her, and in spite of the fact that she was usually a very soft-spoken and kind woman, she told me off in no uncertain terms.

Renee was in the class below mine. When I was still with Mara, Renee and I had sat next to each other on the bus one day and had a really nice conversation. I wasn't particularly attracted to her, but I felt like we clicked, and I wanted to become better friends with her after Mara and I broke up. (I guess in truth, I wanted us to be close friends.) Unfortunately, Renee didn't have the desire to be close to me. Eventually, she felt that I was calling her too much, even though the most I ever called was three times in one week. (Not one of those times did she answer.) After she informed me that she didn't want to be my friend, it didn't sit right because I felt like she misunderstood me (predictably). I wrote her an e-mail trying to get her to talk to me so we could clear the air, and she was not happy about it. She ripped into me, so I ripped into her even worse, in effect calling her a lush (based on things I had heard from some of her classmates). Even if she did have some sort of drinking problem, as those people had said, what right was it of mine to bring it up?

I was wrong in both situations. I knew it with Kara immediately and e-mailed her an apology. I hope she read it. With Renee, it took me a while to see where I had been mistaken. For a long time, I just thought she was nuts and not very nice. I think I apologized to her maybe a year later. A plus is that I did it to her face after we both got off the same bus one morning. She apologized to me in return, and that made me feel a lot better about what had happened. After that, we even chatted in clinic once in a while. We never became "friends," but at least there was no bad blood left between us.

All in all, those two situations were just big misunderstandings. I wanted to make a connection with two women who seemed to me to be pretty good people. But by reaching out, I unwittingly offended them. I wish I could take back everything I did. Given a second opportunity, I would just leave them both alone. I guess there is no use crying over spilt milk.

At some point I had become privy to the fact that Liz (the girl I liked in the first year class) had a boyfriend. Subsequently, my focus drifted away from her. A few months later, before the summer quarter started, I found out that her relationship had ended and she was single again. I did feel as though I was pretty into her. I really liked her personality; she was blunt and honest, motivated and opinionated. She was nice too. I felt that she was exactly the type of person I could get into a meaningful relationship with. I wanted to find out if I was right. When I found out she was single, I made a move. I was somewhat tired of my same old approach at that point, and I was familiar with this woman to an extent, so I decided that I would try something sweeter and more heart-felt. I wanted to make her feel special and hopefully win her affections in the process, so I constructed a plan to be her "secret admirer." If I could build up her anticipation with progressively deeper notes that revealed my feelings and intentions concerning her, I thought there was a good chance that she would appreciate the trouble and start to be swayed by my romantic side. I didn't know how she felt about me, one way or the other, but if there was anything there, I could nourish it and give it reason to grow. I think it was a good plan, but she wasn't having it. Without going into details, I only got the chance to leave two notes in her locker before everything went haywire. I was forced to call her on the phone and confess. I hadn't even had a chance to say anything romantic yet. When we talked, I came clean and we subsequently discussed my desire to date her. She thought we were "too similar." She said that we could date, but she didn't see a future in it. She didn't see any point. I didn't think that being too similar was a good reason not to date someone, but it seemed her mind was set. I didn't have the heart to argue with her that day, for fear of saying something wrong and making myself look bad, so I put up just a small fight and soon conceded. Again, I was left empty-handed, and it was deflating that I didn't get to carry out my plan. Everything was up to her though, and she didn't want to know me any more than she already did. Regretfully, the effort I had spent constructing my plan to impress her had altered me in an unfortunate way, though I would remain unaware for some time.

One more setback... Disheartening, but I kept right on hitting on women that I deemed attractive, wherever I could find them. I dated quite a bit, but I just couldn't catch a break and find anyone that I really meshed with. I had all sorts of failures. One woman I dated was extremely beautiful and intelligent. She seemed nice at first, but I broke it off with her a month into things because she was probably the most self-centered, entitled person I had ever met. Other women I dated were much nicer, but didn't do it for me intellectually. Yet others were beautiful and educated and seemingly nice, but I promptly chased them away with my mixed up, apparently arrogant demeanor. If I was actually intrigued with a woman after learning a little about her, it almost seemed to be a guarantee that she would want nothing to do with me. Once again, I could not reconcile the perceptions of others with who I really was. I tried to keep positive and just play the numbers game, holding onto the idea that I would eventually find the right woman for me. At some point, someone who I was into would appreciate me for who I was. What I just couldn't see was that I wasn't myself, so there was really no chance of another person seeing the truth. My defense mechanisms had walled my true intentions off from the sight of other people, and my isolation grew deeper and deeper.

19

Temporary Insanity

DJ and I have been the very best of friends since our first days together during high school. I know he has my back no matter what may come. It goes without saying that I'll be there for him whenever he needs me. But, as we all know, stress can alter people, if only slightly or temporarily. On a Saturday afternoon during the spring of my third year, DJ found that out the hard way. He had gotten up early that morning to take his car into the mechanic. When I woke up, I wanted to hang out with him, so I gave him a call on his cell phone. When he answered, I asked, "Where you at?" (For those of you who aren't familiar with hip-hop culture in the US, "Where you at?" is a greeting. It doesn't necessarily mean you are trying to determine someone's whereabouts. It's more like saying, "What's up?") After I asked the question, DJ's voice turned sour and he replied with, "Out." I read the change in his tone and immediately took offense at his indignation. "Why you gotta be a dick?" I asked. His response was to ask me why I was trying to keep tabs on him. "You're not my mother," he said. I became really angry at that, and I hung up on him. He called back, and I answered just so I could hang up on him again. Real mature… He got home a few minutes later and came to talk to me. We started to argue in my room, but soon took our battle up the stairs towards the kitchen.

When we got to the top of the stairs, the unpleasantness had escalated into downright nastiness. We stood there, jawing back and forth at each other like children, as our frustration with each other grew and grew until it reached a tipping point. All of a sudden, we were chest to chest and DJ was asking if I was going to hit him. Even at that point, I was in control enough to know that I would regret throwing a punch at my boy, so I said "No." Then DJ asked if I was going to "breathe" on him. I almost laughed… almost. Still, when I'm angry, humor by the offending party almost always makes it worse. (DJ wasn't actually trying to be funny, but it came out that way, so it got under my skin.) Enraged just a little bit more by the question, I swung my shoulder into DJ rather forcefully. He shouldered me back. Then I grabbed him and shoved him into the wall behind him. He responded by resetting himself and shoving me back into the wall just a couple of feet behind me. I shoved back, and he went into his wall once more. He shoved back, and I returned to mine. Then, some instinct in DJ decided that he should get me out of his general vicinity, so he basically threw me down the stairs. "What the hell?!" I thought. That was not going to stand. I caught myself two steps down, reached up and grabbed his shirt, then yanked him as hard as I could right down on top of me. The force that I pulled him with rotated my body one hundred and eighty degrees, and his body landed on my back as we took a rather quick trip down the stairs. It was so fast that I couldn't do anything but try to run under myself. When my socks hit the linoleum floor at the bottom of the stairs, all of DJ's weight was squarely on my shoulders and his feet were off of the ground. We slid across the eight feet of floor and bashed into the wall and doorframe on the other side of it like some sort of clumsy unisex ice-skating tandem. I hit the crest of my right hipbone hard on the doorframe, but adrenaline didn't allow me to feel it right away. DJ and I both crashed down, with me landing on top of his back. As soon as we came to a stop, DJ decided that we should stop acting like idiots before things got worse and he called out, "Wait,

wait!" I just pushed myself off of him, then grabbed the back of his head and shoved it down as I stood up while calling him an expletive. I walked away and into the laundry room next door. DJ got up and followed me in. I was so frustrated at that point that I grabbed this crappy metal shelf that was next to the wall and shook the shelves off of it before slamming the frame into the floor. While doing so I growled loudly in anger. DJ and I looked straight at each other for a second… before bursting into laughter. We had almost killed each other over what? In a word, it was ludicrous.

After showering up, we went downtown and did some browsing at the stores there. While we did, we talked over our duel from earlier in the day. There wasn't an ounce of bad blood. In fact, we both knew that the day's violence had brought us closer, if that was possible. As hard as I was trying to hide my inner turmoil, DJ knew that I was a bit on edge, and he understood my frustrations. He knew I had never intended to hurt him. Neither had he intended to hurt me. There was no question of that. As we were walking across the street to go into the Nike store around dusk, DJ made me laugh. With the laughter, came the pain of another contusion; this time it was in the oblique muscle just above my right hipbone. It was my third contusion in the last two years. I knew the drill. Early morning trips to the tub were on the horizon once again. I guess the severity of this injury wasn't so bad, because it never hurt quite as much in the mornings as the first two had (or maybe I was just used to it by then).

20

Maybe You

Right after my attempts to win Liz's favor failed, I met one of the most impressive women I had ever come into contact with. I was at the university's gymnasium on a Sunday afternoon taking jump shots on the floor second to the top of the building. The top floor was a full-sized track that followed the perimeter of the building and overlooked the basketball courts on the floor below. As I shot around, I noticed a woman running intensely around the track. I could see from where I was that she was in very good shape, and it was also pretty obvious how she got that way. She just kept running and running and running, around and around the track. I was intrigued, and I wanted to get a closer look at her, so I went up to the top floor and started to stretch on one of the mats that were in a little area off the track. When the woman ran by, I got a good look at her. She had a very beautiful face. At that point, I decided that I very much wanted to talk to her. I didn't want to interrupt her, so I figured I would wait until she finished running, then catch up to her on her way to wherever she was going next. All I had to do was make sure I kept track of her whereabouts. Dishearteningly, after a few minutes, I lost sight of her and she ceased passing by my position. I got up and jogged around the track once to see if she was at one of the other open areas on that floor, but she wasn't. Thinking quickly, I decided that I should go get my stuff and hang out by the gym entrance to see if I could catch her on her way out. I was done with my workout anyhow, and I hoped she had gone to the locker room to get ready to leave. Maybe if I moved fast enough, I could "head her off at the pass," so to speak.

When I got to the entrance of the gym, I sat down at one of the tables near the smoothie bar and watched the end of an NBA playoff game. Probably twenty minutes passed, and I was beginning to think that my opportunity had slipped away. The beautiful, fit, intense girl had not come my way, and I decided that I would leave if I didn't see her soon. I figured she had probably left the building before I ever made it to the lobby. For a few minutes, I became distracted by the game and forgot all about the reason I was sitting there in the first place. When I took my gaze away from the TV again, I was startled to find that the woman had reappeared; she had just walked out the entrance and was headed for the parking lot. She was moving at a rapid pace, so I hopped up and walked hastily after her.

I caught up to her maybe a few hundred feet from the parking lot and tapped her on her left shoulder. She turned around, and I promptly delivered the most unassuming pass I could come up with. (I was feeling somewhat more shy than normal that day, so I went for more of a hopeful, asking type of a line.) I somewhat sheepishly told her that I had seen her running around the track and that I "really wanted to meet" her. She took it well, and we made conversation as we walked towards the parking lot. I was happy to learn that she was twenty-four (only a couple of years younger than me) and that she was just about to finish her master's degree in geography. She was beautiful, educated, motivated, and fit. How could it get any better than that? If she wasn't full of herself, she was pretty amazing. I asked her for her phone number, and after she gave it to me, we parted ways. I was happy that I had decided to wait around for her, and I was looking forward to seeing if she was as impressive as she seemed. I really hoped that she was. Her name was Paige.

Things developed slowly with Paige. She didn't answer the first two times I called, and I was forced to leave voicemails. The first was standard, but a week later, when my call was sent to voicemail for the second time, I felt a bit perturbed. I decided that I was going to be very blunt. I told her that I didn't want to seem rude or presumptuous, but that I would really appreciate it if she would get back to me as opposed to not doing so. I understood that she was probably very busy, but it would only take a few minutes to give me a ring and say hi. I really didn't want to be offensive, but I did want to lay a bit of a guilt trip on her. In a way, I think I was trying to get back at all the women who had ignored me after giving me their numbers. Maybe it wasn't the proper thing to do, but I was trying to reach out to these women. I wanted to see who they were, and it always hurt so bad having to figure out that they weren't interested in knowing me by waiting for calls that never came. That was the first time I ever did anything like that, and I really didn't expect it to work, but I was surprised the next day when Paige called and left me a voicemail. She was even apologetic for not getting back to me sooner. She told me that she had been extremely busy because she was finishing up her master's degree and that things were going to be hectic for her for the next few weeks. Even so, she would try to make some time to talk to me if I called back. I thought that the way she handled my message spoke volumes about her.

We talked on the phone for around thirty minutes a few days later. She was a bit shy, but nice. I also got the feeling that she was pretty spunky and independent from some of her reactions to certain things I asked. All in all, we got along well. As she had told me in her voicemail, she was going to be very busy in the immediate future, so we wouldn't get a chance to do anything together for at least a few weeks. I understood, and I told her that I'd give her a call later on when she was done with all of her duties. I was glad to have finally gotten a few minutes to learn a little more about her. She seemed like a solid person, and I wanted to know more about her, for sure.

Maybe a month went by, and I gave Paige a call. I figured that she was probably finished with the bulk of her responsibilities by then. She didn't answer. I left a message, expecting that she would call back within a couple of days. That didn't happen. After about two weeks of waiting, I decided to e-mail her. I didn't have her e-mail address, but that problem was easily fixable. I don't know if it works this way at every university, but at my school, you could look up another student's contact information through the school's website. Now, I realize that doing something like that can definitely make a person look bad, and if certain assumptions are made, even dangerous. Regardless of that, I wanted to communicate with Paige, and writing someone a letter often works better for that than leaving a voicemail. Besides, I wasn't dangerous. I knew that, so if only in my own mind, what I did was justifiable. I hoped Paige would understand. What I said in the letter was simply that I hoped she hadn't decided that she didn't want anything more to do with me and that I really did want to meet up with her and get to know her a bit better. I also told her that she seemed like a really worthwhile woman. I hoped she would write back or call soon. Once again, I was trying to make her feel somewhat guilty, and once again, she got in touch with me and was apologetic. Again, I was impressed by the way she handled the situation. When we spoke next, we set up a time and a place to meet later on in the week.

On the day of our date, I arrived at the restaurant we had chosen to meet at before Paige. I remember thinking how impressive she was when she walked in. She was very beautiful, and in more than just your standard ways. She was so fit. Her turquoise poncho and blue jeans looked so nice on her, perfectly complimenting her dirty blonde hair and fiery hazel eyes. She had such great posture too. Many women have pretty poor posture, but Paige's was perfect. Especially for a woman as tall as her, that is a rare trait. Besides her beauty, she had intelligence and education and intensity. I couldn't help but feel a bit nervous, and I took a deep breath before she sat down. To start off our conversation, we greeted each other as she took the seat across from me.

Things started out really well. Paige asked me how I was doing, and I admitted to her that I was pretty nervous. She said she was too. I was pleased to hear that because it meant she was hopeful. Then we talked about the day we met. To my great surprise, she told me that she had intended to come over and stretch beside me that day. She had noticed me too and thought I was cute. She said she went into the women's restroom for a few minutes, and when she came out, I was gone. She thought she had missed me. I found it difficult at that point to hold back the wide smile that my face was breaking into.

After that, I got right to work at destroying Paige's opinion of me, and it didn't take me too long to do just that. I think my interactions with her that day were a perfect example of why I had such a hard time with women in that city. I talked a lot. I filled the silence. I asked her a lot of questions, but after her short answers, I probably talked twice as much as she did. Some would say that instead of being interestED in her, I was trying to be interestING. It really wasn't anything like that. While my intentions were pure and good, I became a victim of my own bad habits. From what I can tell so far, talking a lot makes a person look full of himself—like he doesn't have any interest in what the other person has to say. I did care, but like I said before, I have a habit of filling silence with words. On top of being a motor mouth, I asked Paige two questions that perhaps, as a precaution, shouldn't be asked on a first date. The first one was borderline—I asked her what her religion was. As it turned out, she had the same basic beliefs that I did. Although it isn't a mandatory thing for me, similar beliefs make a relationship easier to sustain, so I was happy to hear that we shared the same viewpoint. I didn't realize that she was offended by my question, however, until a few minutes later when I asked Paige when she last had a boyfriend. Her face turned instantly sour as she replied with, "You and the personal questions." I was a bit stunned, so I apologized; but being unsure of what my first transgression had been, I inquired as to what I had asked before that was personal. She told me that it was my question about her religion. I was a bit offended at her taking offense to these questions, but it didn't make me not want to know her. I tried to explain that I was a very forward and honest type and that I sometimes asked questions that offended people because I wouldn't be offended by them myself. Maybe she understood, but the damage was already done. It's hard to turn a visceral response around. Paige was reflexively upset by my probing, and even if she could logically understand that I meant no harm by my questions, they played a major part in her perception of who I was. I asked those questions because I wanted to know who she was. I wanted to learn about her and what made her tick. I guess it was too early for that.

We stumbled along uncomfortably for a while after that, but I felt that we recovered and started getting along better about ten or so minutes later. Little did I know… We went for a walk around the shopping center where the restaurant was located after we finished eating. When we parted, I could feel an uneasiness coming from her. I half expected at least the standard non-intimate hug that many women give after a first date, but Paige extended her hand for a handshake instead. We had talked about possibly seeing a movie the next week as we walked around, so I figured that she just wasn't the touchy-feely type. It took about a week for her to inform me that she had dismissed the idea that I was a person who was worth knowing.

I called Paige about three days after the date to chat. She had been out of Veiltown for the weekend to visit friends in the city where she grew up. She was supposed to be back that evening, but she didn't answer her phone. I left another message asking her if she still wanted to see War of the Worlds with Tom Cruise on Thursday night. Maybe I was just dense, but I really expected that she would come out with me again. I thought we had gotten over our awkward few minutes during the date, but as it turned out, only I had. After she didn't call me back by Tuesday night, I wrote her an e-mail, again asking if she was going to come out with me and telling her that I needed to know soon because I was going to make other plans if we weren't going to the movie. Wednesday came and went, and I finally started to "get the hint" as so many women think men should automatically be able to do. I went to school Thursday figuring that I would never hear from Paige again. How rude… At lunchtime, I checked my e-mail to find a disappointing letter. She told me that she thought I was a nice guy and a very honest person, but she couldn't see us ever being more than friends. I sent an e-mail back, conceding and thanking her for her time.

That Friday night, I was lying in bed thinking, as I am apt to do. (I was especially so during the tumult of that period in my life.) I just didn't understand. Paige and I had a lot of things in common, and except for the unwittingly "personal" questions I had asked her, I felt that we had gotten along well enough for another date. I didn't know whether or not she and I could be a couple or love each other or anything like that, but I knew I wanted to find out more about who she was before I made any kind of decision about her. Was patience too much to ask? I once read in a magazine that most women "know" within fifteen minutes of meeting a man whether or not they can ever be in love with him. Of all the silly beliefs I have heard in my life, this one is probably the silliest. (It is definitely one of the most prejudiced and closed-minded.) How on earth can you possibly know the intricacies of someone in fifteen minutes? How after even one whole date could you know for sure that you couldn't have deep feelings for someone? It all just seemed so illogical. I had once been absolutely sure that I could never be in love with Mara. However, once I got to know her and once I understood how she felt about me, I fell in love with her. It didn't last, as I have already explained, but being with her was absolutely worth it and helped make me into a better person. With all of this in mind, I decided I'd try to reason with Paige. I knew it probably wouldn't work, but I had to try because she was so impressive. I needed to see if there was a chance that we could care about each other, even if only as friends. Just making a friend out of her would be worth the effort in my eyes, so I got out of bed and went to my computer.

I tried very hard to appeal to Paige's sense of reason and fairness in my e-mail to her. To sum it up, I told her that I felt that even though we had a rough spot during our date, I didn't think it was fair of either of us to write the other off. I asked that we could hang out five more times. I was sure that if she could give me that time, I could prove to her that we could and would be great friends, if not more. I suggested some things that we could do together to have fun, and I asked her to consider it. I went to bed with a glimmer of hope that the things I said could make a difference. After all, words can be powerful.

Paige wrote back the next day. Her letter read: "Darren, I read your letter and I am sorry, but I must decline." And that was that. Despite my reflexive compulsion to displace the blame away from myself and onto her for being judgmental, I knew deep inside that it was I who had messed up, once again. The best woman I had met in quite a while wanted nothing to do with me. I was rapidly growing numb.

21

Ready to Fight

A lot like most American males, I have always had an aggressive side to me: a side that wants to resolve disputes with threat displays and, if needed, with physical violence. I feel it is one of the worst parts of my nature. I know that after each and every incident in my life where physical violence has become an option, I have felt very remorseful. At times, it has been difficult for me to take the high road and walk away from conflict before it gets dangerous because my pride dictates that a "real man" should be tough and willing to engage in physical combat. In the face of this, I strive every day to overcome my violent side because, truth be told, nothing good comes from violence. Don't get me wrong. Sometimes violence can't be avoided, especially in the case of defending one's self or another. Still, each and every other option should be evaluated and attempted before violence becomes plausible. Naturally, as my sense of happiness and control over my life go, so goes my ability to do the right thing when it comes to conflict. That can at least partially explain why I almost got into a fight with one of the university's best basketball players.

I went down to the gym to shoot some baskets on a Sunday morning for some exercise. I had no intention of playing any games when I got there, but interestingly to me, the shooting guard of the school's basketball team was there; he was going to play pickup with the other guys who were on the courts. He was a very uniquely talented player. (Always announced at five feet nine inches tall, he wasn't even that, but he could jump out of the gym and was extremely quick.) Not only athletic, but just good at basketball in general, he was a first team all conference player. Seeing a chance to do something challenging and fun, I decided to play in the next pickup game. I was hoping that I would be on the opposite team from the superstar so that I could guard him. I got my wish.

As I have mentioned before, I was going to attempt to try out for the NBA after my first year in school. Obviously, I feel I'm a pretty good basketball player. At six feet two inches tall, I can jump pretty high, especially when in basketball shape. In fact, I used to be able to get my elbow to the rim. I wasn't quite at that point then, but I was in good shape nonetheless, and I still figured that I could give my opponent a challenge. You know: make him sweat a little. To make a long story short, I made it just tough enough for him to score that he became angry with me and started throwing mean-spirited insults my way. I'm not saying that I shut him down, but when he took shots, I was in his face; and with my height and athleticism distracting him, he was having trouble getting clean looks. He still made some shots, but I guess he was used to wide-open looks and a higher percentage when he played pickup games with people who weren't college basketball players. I was pretty surprised by his indignation at me actually guarding him. It seems he thought people were just supposed to move out of his way because he was such a stud. (And here I was figuring that he would want to play against someone who wouldn't lie down for him.) After a few of his insults, I realized that he had a real problem with my defense. At first, I tried to reason with him, and I asked him why he was getting so offended at me playing hard against him. He was in no mood to be nice though. Eventually, I got tired of his mouth and decided to get in his face. (Remember now that I was at least seven to eight inches taller than he was.) I told him that I knew who he was, but being who he was didn't give him the right to be so disrespectful. He just mouthed off some more. I tried to walk away twice, but when I did, he would make some remark that brought me back to ask him to say it to my face (which he would not do). The whole time, I was really just an inch away from laying him on his back for a nap. (I'm not necessarily saying that I would have won a fight with this kid. Although he was small in stature, he was known for being extremely strong, and he grew up in a rough neighborhood where I'm sure he learned to protect himself well. I am just saying that this is how I felt at the time.) Since I knew that knocking out the school's sports hero would not be a smart move for my safety and could also leave me in a legal battle, I finally decided that I was going to leave. I did have some things to lose, for sure. Thinking more clearly, I even tried to tell him that we were both being stupid and that I really didn't have anything against him. He didn't care. Not being a punk was more important to him than accepting the hand of someone reaching out to him to put an end to a conflict, I guess. But how could I blame him? He was twenty-one and I was twenty-six. Five years can make a hell of a difference. I ended up walking away before things got really ugly. As I left, I thought to myself how bad I must have made myself look jawing with that kid. The prideful, aggressive part of me felt like a punk, but the better part of me was pleased. I'm glad I listened to that part.

22

Changing Faces

When our lease was about to end, Errol decided that he wanted to get his own place. DJ and I were okay with it, and we decided to rent a small house in the university district in order to be closer to school and to cut down on commuting. Right at the tail end of our moving process, during the five-week summer break before my final year in dental school, I had major elective surgery. Before that surgery, I had what was called class III malocclusion. That means that I had a permanent underbite (i.e. my lower jaw stuck out further than my upper jaw). In school, we learned that less than one percent of the world's population had such a deformity, and less than one eighth of those people had the deformity severe enough to warrant surgical correction. I was lucky alright… I'm not complaining though. Before the surgery, I was by no means abnormal looking. In fact, the structure of my face did a very nice job of camouflaging my abnormality. Indeed, not even people in the dental field could tell if I didn't show them my teeth and the way they fit together. Before I had started dental school, I never gave that issue much thought. I didn't really care about having a proper bite or even straight teeth. (Mine were extremely crowded.) But a funny thing happens with education: eliminating your ignorance on a certain subject often teaches you to value things related to that subject. After learning a bit about how the human jaws should fit together and especially why they should fit together that way, I began to desire straight teeth and an overbite like "normal" people had. Besides, a dentist with jacked up teeth probably doesn't have much credibility—something like a man teaching a class on feminism. After the end of first year, I had begun what turned out to be a three-year process. It commenced with filling my eight cavities, then progressed to braces for what was supposed to be about eleven months, and finally culminated in orthognathic (literally mouth-straightening) surgery. The process would have only taken around two years, but when I was first scheduled to go through the surgery, I was at the end of a lengthy bout with some unknown upper respiratory infection. I didn't ever get diagnosed, but I was suspicious that I had caught whooping cough because right before my symptoms showed up, there had been a documented case of it on the campus. Whooping cough is a highly contagious disease, so it was not unreasonable for me to believe I might have it. The cough I had sounded different than any I had ever had or heard before, and the description I read of whooping cough matched up very well. At any rate, the cough had lost it's whooping sound by the time I went in for surgery, but I still had a lot of congestion in my sinuses and a less unique sounding cough which produced a fair amount of a lovely yellow-green mucous. The anesthesiologist came in to talk to me right before I was supposed to go under, and she advised me that if I were her son, she wouldn't want me to have surgery that day. There's no more of a ringing endorsement for not doing something than that, as far as I'm aware.

With that, I had to wait eight more months to have the surgery. I wouldn't have felt much like dealing with school for at least two to three weeks after they flayed me open and moved my face around, so I waited for our next extended break to undergo the procedure. When the day came, I calmly went to the local hospital to undertake a major change. When I was a child, I hated the way I looked. I thought I was terribly ugly, and I wished every day that I could have a new face. Eventually, I had come to be at peace with my appearance, and I no longer felt like I was ugly (at least most of the time). It was interesting to me that I was finally going to get what I had wanted so badly as a boy.

About five hours after the anesthesiologist told me to count backward from ten and I had gotten to nine, I awoke in my hospital room. Expectedly, my face felt strange. The surgery entailed completely cutting my upper and lower jaws off of the rest of my skull and resetting them in places that would give me the proper bite with titanium plates and screws. Regrettably, when this is done, there is no way to avoid cutting right through the sensory nerves that supply the jaws and certain areas of the face. Due to that fact, I could not feel anything on the outside of my face from my nose to my chin, and my teeth and gums were completely numb as well. I also had what is called a "chin advancement." This was to make up for the fact that I was going to lose chin prominence because my lower jaw was to be set back two millimeters. The chin advancement entailed cutting the very end of my chin off and setting it forward six millimeters with a titanium plate. I ended up with some long lasting nerve damage from that part of the procedure, although it eventually got better. My face was quite swollen for a few days afterwards, but compared to the faces of most people who underwent the procedure, it was barely swollen at all. I was thankful for that. The literature on the subject says that healthier people swell less and so do males. I was glad to be both of those things.

I was released from the hospital the day after my surgery. DJ came to get me, and when he saw my face, naturally, he burst into laughter. Thanks a bunch, D… We took a trip to Trader Joe's that evening, but I decided to spend most of the next few days at home. I felt like I had been run over by a herd of wombats, so I didn't fancy the idea of leaving the house much. DJ helped take care of me as much as I needed, although that wasn't much. It wasn't like I was incapacitated. I was merely fatigued and had a general feeling of malaise. General anesthesia is a mother… In the past, this sort of surgery required the patient's jaw to be wired shut and the drinking of food through a straw. With the current technology, the need for that was eliminated as titanium plates and screws provided the necessary strength and stability. I was glad for that because I think if I would have had to drink a steak through a straw, the outcome would have been pretty disturbing. If your jaw is wired shut, things have just as difficult of a time getting out as they do getting in, if you catch my drift. As it was, I only had to keep my teeth rubber-banded together when I wasn't eating so as to limit movement, therefore preventing unnecessary discomfort. When I ate, I decided that I would have the best shot at keeping my weight at a reasonable level by eating things that were soft, tasted good, and were also high in calories. To that end, my diet consisted of macaroni and cheese and chocolate milkshakes for about a week. It was every little boy's dream. By the time the week was over and I could start eating a more balanced diet again, I had only lost about ten pounds. I gained five of it back in the next couple of days. Not bad.

You would think that a surgery like that would cause a pretty good amount of pain; but I can honestly say that the only thing I can liken to pain that I ever felt as a result of the surgery was an intense tingling sensation when I tried to shave my Grizzly Adams beard off about five days into recovery. Not pleasant, but I wouldn't have called it pain. Otherwise, I only felt discomfort. That mostly had to do with pressure. When I first came out of surgery, I felt absolutely nothing. I figured that the nerves would start transmitting pain as they gradually reattached themselves, but they never did. Nevertheless, the pressure I felt for about four days was very distracting. It seemed to me that when I first came out of the surgery, my face was swollen enough to compress the nerves into a state of dormancy where they couldn't function to produce any sensation. As the swelling went down and the nerves reattached, they began to function again; but still being partially crushed by the swelling, the first thing they could transmit to the brain was the sensation of pressure. Luckily, I had an ample supply of ibuprofen to decrease the swelling and get me to sleep at night.

All in all, it really was a pretty easy recovery, and I quickly resumed normal activities. (Well, except for weight lifting, which I wasn't allowed to participate in for three months.) I even went with DJ back to the other house to meet Errol for the final cleanup.

23

Lashing Out

Overall, living with Errol had been a good experience. There were a couple of times when I had woken him up and he had gotten upset; and we had also gotten into some pretty heated debates about politics. Generally speaking though, we had lived together well. Errol even bought us two tickets to one of the local NFL team's games as an early Christmas gift to me, and we had also gone to another later that same season. He was a good person. Sometimes, I'm sure Errol grew frustrated with me, and I could definitely say the same in regards to him. Regardless, I never had any intention of ridding myself of his friendship. It was one of the few good things in the sea of bad that I had been floating on.

I think that what happened between us was just a product of my overwhelming unhappiness. In truth, I regret it very much. Unfortunately, an issue arose with our landlord concerning the bathroom door. Errol had tripped and fallen into the door a few months before we left, and his hand put a big hole in it. The door was not repairable and needed to be replaced. Errol gave our landlord money for a new door, and he bought one and brought it over to the house. He wanted us to install the door, and then he would come over and paint it afterwards. Fair enough, right? Well, it ended up taking Errol and DJ considerable effort to make the door fit onto the hinges. (I can't remember exactly why at this point, but they were very glad to be done with it.) Unfortunately, the problems didn't stop there. When the landlord came over and painted the door, the layer of paint he put on made the stupid thing too big to fit into the frame without peeling the paint off the edges. Now, you would think that because the landlord had measured the door and the frame and picked the door out at the home improvement store, he would have taken responsibility for the mistake he made in not calculating the thickness of the paint he was going to apply. Nope. He wanted us to fix the problem. If we didn't, he was going to take money out of our deposit. I have always been a person of principle by my own estimation, but by that point I had decided that not every battle of principle was necessarily worth fighting (especially if it would take time out of one's life). Sometimes, principle isn't worth as much as time. Errol didn't want to fix the door. He was sure that it was the landlord's responsibility and that we hadn't even been obligated to install the thing. He would not budge. I didn't want to lose part of the deposit or have to go through any unpleasantness to keep it. I figured that, in the interest of saving time and effort, we should just fix the door and get our money back. DJ agreed that doing so would save us all from a hassle while also protecting our rental histories. Besides, our landlord had been very nice to us and fair during the year we had been there, so neither of us saw any reason to put any strain on the relationship.

DJ and I pulled the door off the frame and took it down to our new place in the university district so we could modify it. All we had to do was sand down the edges so our landlord could repaint them, and that would be that. What was insulting about it was that Errol refused to even help us. He said he was putting his foot down because it wasn't our responsibility. If he had to, he would even go to court over it. Imagine: he would be willing to litigate over maybe a hundred and fifty dollars. I couldn't believe it. At the very least, because the deposit was part mine and part DJ's, I just figured that the nice thing to do would have been to help us out when we made the decision that we were going to get it back without a hassle. I couldn't afford to wait for my share of the cash, and I felt that Errol should have understood that as opposed to preferring to put us through some waste-of-time legal battle. It may have been an accident, but Errol broke the damn door in the first place! In spite of that, I was willing to let it go. It pissed me off, but I figured I could get over it.

After DJ and I reinstalled the door and the landlord painted it to discover that it fit correctly, he agreed to give back all of the deposit. At least that was over with. He would send the check to Errol, and Errol would give DJ and I our shares from there. I had no reason to believe any problems would arise from that point on. I was wrong. Unfortunately for both Errol and myself, I forgot an important detail about the pet deposit. When we moved in, Errol had decided that he would pay more of the required amount even though he only owned one third of the dogs. (Errol had a black labrador named Sammy.) He wanted to get more back when we moved out, thus using the landlord as a sort of a savings account. I agreed at the time, figuring I would remember. When Errol received the check from the landlord (a few weeks after my surgery), he called and reminded me of this fact. I, already being a bit upset at the way Errol hadn't helped DJ and I handle the door situation, couldn't fathom how his description of what happened could possibly be true. He was so frugal with his money that it seemed utterly ridiculous that he would offer to pay more of the deposit when I had more dogs. Rather than remaining calm and trying to get all of the info so I could actually think about it, I used what I thought was Errol being a greedy jerk as an excuse to go off on him. Even with only partially healed and somewhat immobilized jaws, I ripped into him for being a "tightwad" and also for being too damn stubborn about silly things (namely the door). He told me that his check register showed the amount he had put in for the deposit and I could see it if I wanted. In actuality, I was starting to recall that he was telling the truth, but I was already too far into my tirade to give a damn about that anymore. The door was the real issue, and with it, all of the aspects of Errol's personality that rubbed me the wrong way. (Those happened to include how, when I told him about my little episode with the college basketball star, he made the judgment that I must have caused the whole thing. How do you take the side of a complete stranger over that of a good friend, especially when you didn't actually see what happened?) I definitely got a little carried away. By the end of my rant, I told Errol that I thought he was the pettiest person I had ever met and that we weren't friends anymore. Then I hung up. What an awful thing to do to a friend. But I was too wounded to understand what I had just done. Somehow, I felt justified and even happy to be rid of him.

Over the year, I had continued to spend time with Steve as well. DJ had known Steve two years longer than I had, and all four of us, including Errol, would get together and hang out from time to time. Steve and I had begun to grow apart though. It seemed that whenever we disagreed about something, he would insult my intelligence. It is true that Steve had probably the most gifted intellect I have ever come into contact with, but even if he was somewhat smarter than me in some ways, I didn't appreciate the condescending tones he often took with me. It wasn't like I was some idiot; after all, I was getting a doctoral degree. Steve had this issue that didn't allow him to admit he was ever wrong, even if you could prove it to him beyond the shadow of a doubt. That eventually led to the demise of our friendship.

After I had cut things off with Errol, Steve and I went to see a movie one night with his roommate. Later in the evening, we had a disagreement about some TV show. I didn't want to argue about it, so I just let Steve have his little victory. Still, I went home determined to prove him wrong. It didn't take long for me to find the bit of evidence I needed. A few days later, as we chatted over the Internet, I presented it in an effort to prove to Steve that he had been mistaken. He got mad at me for that, claiming that I was always trying to prove him wrong. He said he was tired of it. I told him that I was only trying to prove him wrong so often because he always had to be right; he never let anyone else's viewpoint or any information they might present into the equation. I knew he was smart, but it

114

seemed extremely pompous to me that he didn't even respect the input of his friends, who were all very intelligent and educated as well. (He had even argued with me about dentistry and with DJ about economics.) He wasn't willing to take any blame, as was usually the case, so our conversation escalated into me belittling him based on the fact that he was overweight and unhealthy. I definitely wasn't anything close to nice or constructive with my criticisms. After bandying insults around for a while, I realized that I had acted in anger and tried to apologize. Regrettably, the damage was already done. We have spoken maybe two or three times since that day.

24

Creating Reasons

The more I failed in my dating life, the more I could feel myself change inside. I had always been hopeful and romantically idealistic when it came to matters of love. I have already relayed how I had become skeptical at the end of my relationship with Mara, but quickly discovered that it was only a temporary problem. After I realized that I still valued love above all other things, finding it once again took priority. But with each failure and each time I was written off on a first impression, a little bit of the hope I carried for a life of love and happiness died. I started to believe that I was actually not anything that a good woman would want: not funny, not charismatic, not attractive. Still, I didn't want to give up my search. Maybe it was a test. Maybe if I kept trying, everything would turn out okay. While I was recovering from surgery, I lamented that there was no woman who would make me a milkshake when I felt too dizzy to stand for long or whose lap I could fall asleep on when the lingering effects of the anesthesia brought on early exhaustion, and my ability to stay conscious waned. As I healed, day-by-day, I hoped that the change in my face would bring about a new attitude and some new luck with it. My loneliness had gotten much worse after Liz and

Paige, but I only partially understood the ways in which it was affecting me. I kept a stiff upper lip and forced myself to keep on believing that if I kept trying, I would find someone to be with and to love. At the same time, I knew that I was in the middle of a dangerous period. I had a strong suspicion that if I were to be turned away too many more times (even though it might be unintentional), I would lose my optimism about dating; I wouldn't be able to open my heart to the possibility that any given woman might be right for me. As the loneliness and dejection inside of me grew, with them grew the skepticism that I could ever find what I desired... what I needed. The interplay of those things caused an overwhelming sort of desperation, and it led me to do one thing in particular that I'm not so proud of.

I guess in a way, my need for affection had pushed me to a breaking point. My heart reached for something solid to grasp onto as I spiraled down into a world of self-criticism and despair. DJ and Darren eased my passage the best they could, but there were some things that they just couldn't provide. Only committed, romantic love could give me what I needed, and the lack of it was causing the hole in me to grow faster by the day. Reflexively, I kept putting a positive spin on things, never truly accepting how sad I had become. Even so, as despair crept further and further in, my judgment became clouded. I wish I could have made it through my life without being able to say that I have actively tried to steal another man's girlfriend. Regrettably, I cannot.

Liz had found herself a boyfriend since my little gambit to win her affections. He was another student in her class at the dental school. I didn't know him, although we had met a couple of times before. Regardless of that, trying to pull her away from him was nothing short of inexcusable. Honestly, I didn't have anything against him, but loneliness and the will to persist pushed me into an emotional state where I could justify what I did with the idea that I would be a better boyfriend to Liz than he was. My previous efforts to impress her had left a bad taste in my mouth, and every time I saw her I felt somewhat bitter. I wanted to prove to her how special I was and how happy she would be with me.

Creating Reasons

Humans have a habit of trying to make things congruent in their own minds. It would be hard to make sense of some of the things we do if this tendency didn't exist. Basically, if we spend a bunch of effort and time on something, we need to have a good reason why—especially if those efforts end in failure. For me, the effort I put forth trying to impress Liz was only justifiable if I actually felt very strongly about her. Around that, I concocted some romantic idea that we should be together, even though deep inside I didn't really feel that way. I had even noticed a few things about her that I really didn't like since she had decided not to date me, but I rationalized them away. In reality, those things would have driven me nuts, given an opportunity for us to be a couple. In my desperate state, I ignored my reservations and tried to start a dialogue with her so I could tell her... I don't know what I wanted to tell her. It all seems so stupid now, and I wish I could take it back. I am telling you about it because it is a good example of how pressure and pain can make a person see things where they aren't and do things that he shouldn't. Hope only knows how to hope—to believe that there is something better. My hope was rapidly fading away, but if it still existed, it was going to do it's best to save me.

The way Liz handled the whole situation was nothing less than mature and classy. Instead of running away and ignoring it or blabbing to the whole school about what an idiot I was, she confronted me and addressed my overtures. She let me know kindly, but in no uncertain terms, that she was happy with her boyfriend and that she wasn't going to entertain my advances. I had no choice but to stop. Truthfully, it was a relief that she made me because the reasons I went forward weren't right. Like I said before, deep down inside, I wasn't so into her (although it took a while to admit it to myself). I was lonely, and I was trying to justify to myself the effort and thought I had put into trying to date her. Yes, I was attracted to her in many ways, but not completely, and I didn't really think she was the answer. I just wanted to feel so badly. I needed to be devoted to something—to have a reason. To that end, I created feelings that were maintained only by pride and an inflated sense of optimism spawned as a last-ditch defense mechanism against the sheer force of the fear that then resided firmly in my heart.

Still, at the end of the day, I had been rejected again. This time it had been by a woman that I at least fooled myself into believing I cared about. Even if I could have understood what actually happened, I don't think it would have changed my psyche's instinctive response to one failure too many. I could feel it come over me, seeping into every recess: a nasty, jaded, hopeless feeling. My last bit of optimism had fallen to the ground and shattered into a million splinters. My emotional defenses were firmly set. They would never allow me to be so open again.

25

Deliverance

I remember the first time I saw her… I don't imagine I'll ever forget it. Greatly ironic and true to life, at first, I did not realize what exactly I was looking at. It had been a little over two months since my surgery, and disregarding my surgeon's advice, it had been over a month since I had started lifting weights again. I hate being out of shape. During the first month after surgery, I felt absolutely disgusting as my heart and muscles got progressively weaker. I couldn't stand being inactive for another second, so I started to lift after the month passed. I never went too heavy or for too long, and I tried extremely hard not to clench my jaw while I lifted, for fear of displacing it and ending up with a crooked smile. By the end of my first month back, I was physically starting to feel more myself again, although I was extremely weak in comparison to earlier times. I didn't really look it though, so at least I had that going for me. The swelling in my face was almost completely gone, and I was feeling pretty good about my appearance.

It was a weeknight, some time around nine o'clock, and I was doing dumbbell biceps curls on a bench in front of the mirrors where all the dumbbells were racked. I noticed a blond-haired woman pass behind me. As I am always likely to do, I repositioned my gaze in the mirror to get a better look at her. She was… unique. She had muscular arms and legs, strong shoulders, and a beautiful neck. Unappealingly, she also had a rather large gut that was round and smooth— a lot like a pregnant woman's, but smaller. Compared to the rest of her, it looked rather out-of-place. The other parts of her body were those of an athlete, but her stomach looked like it belonged to a couch potato or to someone who drinks a little too much. As for her face, I thought it was pretty ugly. She had a bunch of large freckles, and I wasn't impressed with her features: not her eyes, not her mouth, not her cheeks nor her chin. After I had gotten my fill of her and decided consciously that she wasn't up to par, I refocused on my curls. As I continued on, I noticed in the mirror that she was looking in my direction. After a few seconds, she looked again. She actually looked a few more times after that. My thoughts at that point were not very nice. I remember thinking, "Please don't look at me." I've often conceived it is very possible that the powers that be decided to teach me a lesson that day, using her as the instrument.

It has always been peculiar to me what unfolded in my mind after that. From that point, I would see her at the gym every once in a while. She was often with a young-looking set of twin girls. Even though my initial evaluation of her physical beauty was less than kind, I noticed that whenever she was around, I was particularly aware of it. If I was in the same room as her, I found that not only did I want to look at her, I couldn't keep my eyes away. If I had seen her and she had left the room, I always wondered if she had gone home; truthfully, even somewhat unknown to me, I hoped that she hadn't.

I just couldn't wrap my mind around it. I didn't spend too much time thinking about it when I wasn't at the gym or on days when I hadn't seen her, but it was there. Something… Sometimes I would forget myself and stare at her for quite a while as she exercised across the room. I would snap out of it and wonder, "Why are you looking at this girl?" That went on for about three months. I probably saw her around five or six times during that period.

Deliverance

The first time I had seen her had been right around the time that I was trying to replace Liz's boyfriend, so at first, my focus was elsewhere. After that, with my newest wound still fresh and my numbness reaching a crushingly high level, I was loath to entertain the idea of having feelings for any woman. If asked at the time, I would have maintained fervently that I was not at all interested in dating this woman. I was completely out of hope. Even though I was very skeptical that it could happen, I had always desired that I would experience a strong, instant reaction to someone that would ultimately lead to something amazing. Perhaps you could call it "love at first sight." I had convinced myself that I felt that for Liz, but after the debacle with her, I was absolutely certain that my heart was incapable of feeling that sort of foolish emotion ever again. My skepticism had grown extremely strong, as a natural result of so many failed attempts taken with such untainted optimism. Failure can only be endured so many times before even the most steadfast spirit will begin to grow hesitant. Even though I knew it wasn't a positive way to be, I doubted very seriously that I had the fortitude to ever leave myself vulnerable to such disappointment again. With that in mind and heart, it was a laughable notion that this out-of-shape, ugly woman could somehow open me up again. As a way of explaining my fixation with her to myself, I half came to the conclusion that looking at her was like looking at a car-wreck for me: I really didn't want to see, yet I had enough morbid curiosity to draw me in. I was fooling myself.

Then one day in December, things abruptly took a step in the direction of clarity. I walked into the gym on a Sunday afternoon and made my way to the check-in counter. As I was fiddling around in my bag to get my student ID out, I noticed a woman with an incredibly fit and beautiful body walk by me on her way out of the building. When I looked at her face, I was stunned to find that she was that same out-of-shape, ugly girl that I could never keep my eyes off. At first I couldn't believe that I was looking at the same woman. Nevertheless, I had noticed a little brown mark on one of that girl's thighs, and as sure as day, it was on this girl's thigh too. I hadn't seen her in maybe a month or more, and she had made some changes. Any extra weight that she had been carrying previously was long gone. I can't imagine what the look on my face must have been. I wish I could have somehow seen. As I checked in and continued down the hall towards the stairs, I looked back to see her walking away. That was the day that everything started to change for me.

All throughout that workout, my mind was on one thing: her. Now, instead of wondering why I wanted to look at a woman that I wasn't attracted to, I was thinking of reasons why I shouldn't talk to her. It wasn't as if I was afraid to. On the contrary. At the time, I still viewed myself as the one in control of the situation. I was convinced that she was at least physically attracted to me from past observation. If I wanted to, it would be easy for me to get a date. I was against the idea of asking though, because I had put something together in my head. She didn't look particularly young, but I was relatively certain that she was at least five years younger than me. Few women were that fit and muscular without having a competitive reason. In my mind, the only possible explanations were that she competed in fitness/figure pageants, or she was a college athlete. Generally speaking, fitness/figure competitors don't train at college gymnasiums, so she had to be an athlete. That meant that if she was a senior, she could be a maximum of twenty-two years old. If she wasn't a senior, she would be younger. Either way, I couldn't talk to her. I was twenty-seven. I couldn't date a twenty-two-year-old. And what if she was younger? What if she was only a sophomore or a freshman? That just wouldn't do. I had always thought guys who dated women who were that much younger than them were sleazebag perverts. The last thing I wanted to do was join THAT club. I'd never forgive myself.

I wanted to find out her age, if only so I could stop wondering, so when I went home that day, I did what any red-blooded, curious American boy who grew up in the information age would do: I looked her up on the Internet. I went to the university's athletics website and started to look through the rosters of the women's teams to see if I could find her. It didn't take long. I tried two other sports before I got to gymnastics. The very first profile I clicked on was hers. The picture looked somewhat different, so I took the name and searched for it on Google. I looked at a few different pictures that came up, and I still wasn't completely sure. Soon I found a picture that cleared up any confusion. In the picture, that little brown mark was plainly visible on her thigh. Next, I went back and read her profile. She was a junior and would turn twenty-one in March. There you had it. I just couldn't date a girl who was seven years younger than me; that would be at odds with my principles. Besides, I still thought her face was ugly. Too much about the situation was out of whack. I decided that I would just forget it. Unbeknownst to me, that decision wasn't mine to make. That would soon become abundantly clear.

During finals week that quarter, I spent a lot of time at the gym. Senior dental students don't really have finals—some sort of sarcastic reward after getting our asses handed to us for three years. At any rate, I wanted to start being more intense about my workouts since my healing process after surgery was pretty far along. I felt that my muscles were ready for more work, so I went to the gym Monday through Friday. I saw that woman just about every day. It seemed like everywhere I looked, there she was. I couldn't keep my eyes off her... especially then. She was so graceful... like a gazelle, but subtle like water or wind. I was fighting it as hard as I could, but just seeing her walk by was driving me nuts. I had never seen anyone who moved like that. By and large, she was definitely different from how she had been the first few times I had seen her, yet she was the same. What I mean to say is she had this energy about her: this vibe... I think it was there before, only much more difficult for me to detect.

By Wednesday, my resolve was crumbling away in large chunks. That day, she wore all red. Red was absolutely her color (not to mention my favorite). Thinking back, I can actually pinpoint the very second that the last of my defenses came down. She used to do abdominal exercises in a corner of the weight room: some Pilate-type stuff and crunches and such. I was walking by that area after getting some water from the fountain, and I glanced over at her. She was looking in my direction at that moment, and our eyes met. I was still trying to keep myself from talking to her, so I just turned away and kept walking. A second later though, my neck muscles independently made the decision that my eyes hadn't seen enough, and they turned my head one hundred and eighty degrees to look back at her. She was, oh, five feet behind me, walking the same direction. And she saw… I turned around feeling a bit embarrassed. I just sort of shook my head and kept going about my business. I can't remember making a conscious decision to look back at her. It just happened before I could do anything to stop it.

I think that most of the transformation we undergo throughout our lives is gradual, but every once in a while, a moment in time comes along that alters us dramatically and permanently. For me, that moment was one of those moments. They have been very rare in my life to this point, but I guess you could even call it a moment of clarity. There, before my eyes, was that something. Right there—as bright and as undeniable as the sun. In a split second, something inside of me opened. A switch flipped. The hammer hit… and I was forever changed. When I looked back at her, I saw her face as beautiful for the very first time, and I became acutely aware that I had never been so completely and utterly attracted to someone. I suppose it was just a matter of realizing it. Now, when I thought about all those times I had spent sneaking glances and sometimes just staring, even before she got in shape, I understood. Instantly, the fact that she was seven years younger than me ceased to matter, and more so than my mind, my heart was made up.

26

Paralysis

Some things in life are necessarily easier said than done. The instant that I started
to realize what I was feeling for this woman, the thought of talking to her became
extremely nerve-wracking. I saw her twice more that week, and I couldn't bring
myself to talk to her. I didn't see her again for a week after that (most likely
because she went home for Christmas). Then I saw her three or four more times
before school started up in early January. Still, I couldn't do it. I had flat-out hit
on probably forty to fifty women since I had broken up with Mara. Most of them
had been very beautiful, and I just walked up and said what I had to say. Yeah, I
was somewhat nervous each time, but it wasn't a big deal. Suddenly, I was
absolutely terrified of trying to talk to this one friggin' woman. I couldn't
understand it. How could this be that hard for me? All I had to do was walk up
and say hi. Then we would have a quick little conversation, I would find out if
she was single, and the rest would take care of itself. Why would it be any
different from what I had gone through in the past? But the opportunities kept on
coming, and I kept on letting them slip by without so much as smiling at her.

By then, I had unintentionally learned her exercise routine, so I knew where she would be sequentially. (It wasn't like I was standing there going, "Okay. Now, after she runs, she will go use the Swiss ball." I just picked it up.) A couple of times, I put myself on the Stairmaster next to the one that she liked to use five or ten minutes before she finished her circuit training on the treadmill. I should have said something one of those times, but I couldn't; my lips wouldn't move. I would just step and step until she finished and went downstairs to work on her abs.

Every time an opportunity passed, I got a little angrier with myself. I was stalling when I needed to be taking action. I kept telling myself that she was single, and if I waited too long, somebody else would snatch her away. No matter who he was, that guy wouldn't be able to treat her the way I would, so I couldn't let that happen. I had to talk to her, regardless of how hard it was. On the last Friday before school started, she came into the gym with a bunch of her teammates. I could tell because they all had chalk on their thighs. I had never thought that chalk could be an accessory to an outfit, but it made her even that much more beautiful to me. I positioned myself on the Stairmaster once again, but I didn't say anything as she worked through her interval. However, I did make up my mind that she wasn't leaving the building without me talking to her. No more stalling. I had planned to get at her downstairs after she finished her abs, but she left early without doing them. STUPID! I wasted another opportunity. She was right there next to me and I punked out. Again! I came into the gym the next day in hopes that she would come in, but she and her teammates had left Veiltown for their first meet of the season.

I wondered if I had completely blown any chance I ever had with her. School was starting back up the next week, and I remembered that I didn't see her that many times before winter break. My days would be full, and I would only be able to get in to the gym at night. I had no clue what her schedule would be like. I hoped desperately that I would see her again, before any chance that I might have was gone. I went to the gym every day for the next two weeks,

Saturdays and Sundays included, grasping at the hope that she would be there. I wouldn't let her walk away again. No way… I swore that to myself with every second that passed. The days went by, and my muscles grew stronger, but my sadness did too. I was so filled with regret. I was going to die without even drawing my knife. I let all those chances pass me by. How could I have been so hesitant?

One night in the middle of the second week of school, I left the gym after it had gotten dark. Once again, she had not been there. It was raining pretty hard that night, and my mind was absolutely swimming in a sea of frustration. As I passed by, I remember looking up at the sky above the intramural soccer fields. The field's lights were on, illuminating the falling drops of water as they sped towards the ground. It was an amazing sight. I stopped walking and turned my head towards the sky. As hundreds of raindrops hit me about the eyes and mouth, I closed my eyes, and my heart let out a prayer. "Please give me one more chance to get this right. Don't let me fail this way… as a coward." As I opened my eyes, the falling rain splashed into them, stinging with each drop. I didn't turn away. I kept my eyes open. The pain of the rain was nothing compared to what I had been through and what I was going through then. After a long time, I began to shiver. I made my way home through the downpour and changed clothes to turn in for the night.

The weekend came and went, again, without her being at the gym when I was. DJ and I had been planning a snowboarding trip with some of his friends from the economics program that Monday (which was Martin Luther King Day). Not surprisingly, my mind was too troubled for me to get to sleep at a reasonable hour. When it came time to wake up for the drive to the mountains, I had caught a grand total of two hours of sleep. I decided to stay home. I really wanted to go; indeed, I had been looking forward to it. I was just so exhausted though. DJ grudgingly left me to my own devices and took off for the slopes.

I woke up around eleven AM and subsequently prepared myself to go to the gym. When I got there, I lifted for two hours. Next, I did some cardio for an hour and a half. I was just trying to hang around long enough to give her a chance to come in. For some reason, I was feeling pretty confident that day. It was going to be a snap. If she came in, I would sweep her off her feet. She didn't have a chance. Disappointingly, three and one half hours of exercise time went by, and she still hadn't shown up. I had run out of things to do, so I went downstairs to the locker room and took a shower. I took my time. Then I got dressed into my street clothes. I had pretty much given up on her coming in as I dejectedly sulked my way up the stairs to the ground floor. What a waste… But that day, my prayer would be answered in the form of my own insomnia. As I reached the top of the stairs and looked toward the main cardio room at the front of the facility, my eyes focused on that unmistakable silhouette. Game on. With that, all my confidence took the fastest train it could, right out of town.

Maybe it was the fact that I knew I wasn't going to leave without talking to her that turned my legs to gelatin. For certain, I was a mess. I walked over to the smoothie bar in the lobby as hastily as I could and asked for my standard drink. When I went to pay the woman running the cash register, I was distraught to find that my hand was shaking; and it was very visible. The cashier noticed too, and she gave me a questioning look. I just sort of smiled sheepishly and went to sit at the bar to wait for my smoothie. "Get it together! She's just a girl…" I held my hands up in front of my face and watched them tremble like leaves. It had to stop. I closed my eyes and tried to calm myself, logically re-analyzing the situation, but also reiterating to myself that I didn't have the leeway to be nervous at the moment. This was important, and I knew it well. My meditation was interrupted by my drink being placed in front of me. As I opened my eyes, I could feel myself calming down. I reached for the cup and saw that my hands were still shaking, but much less than before. I took a deep breath as I inserted my straw into the lid. I took a few sips and breathed in slowly, out slowly, in slowly, out slowly. "Thank God…" I was alright.

From where I was seated, I could look outside through the windows, across the main walkway leading into the building, and into the cardio room through the window there. Through the glare of the daylight bouncing off the windows, I could barely make her out as she ran on the treadmill. I didn't want to interrupt her in the middle of training, so I decided that I would wait until she left that machine and moved to the Stairmaster. It would be about ten minutes before that happened. If I somehow didn't get to her before she started, I definitely intended to interrupt her then. I would not miss this chance for any reason. When I figured I had about five minutes left, I got up and went downstairs to the locker room. I drank as much of my drink as I could before I got there, but ended up trashing more than three fourths of it. I really didn't know why I bought it anyhow. I think I wanted to appear like I had some reason to be there if she saw me. Perhaps I had forgotten that I DID have a reason, even without the smoothie: I was there to exercise. Imagine that. When I got to the locker room, I went to the mirror and examined myself closely. I took a paper towel and wiped the shine off my face, then checked my nose for boogers. A friend of mine in high school once told me that she had been attracted to a guy until he had the misfortune of talking to her without knowing that he had a big chunk of snot in one nostril. After that, she wanted nothing to do with him. Wouldn't that be a cruel twist of fate? I couldn't let a little oversight like that do me in. When I was sure I was clean and ready to go, I looked at myself one last time to see if I thought I looked attractive. I didn't feel my best, but there was nothing I could do about it. The time had come. I was even starting to feel excited about what was about to happen, as opposed to just nervous. I smiled at myself and turned to go.

As I walked up the stairs and the moment grew closer, the nervousness again intensified. I was locked in though. Neither nervousness nor doubt would keep me from doing what I had to do. I was so emotionally spent from two weeks of hoping fruitlessly that she would be at the gym when I went. The thought of going through that for another indefinite period was far more terrifying than the thought of anteing up and just talking to her. I got to the top of the stairs, then turned and walked toward the door that led into the part of the cardio room where the Stairmasters were. When I entered, she wasn't at the machine yet. "Screw it."

I kept walking, intending to go to the treadmill where I had seen her or catch her on her way. There was a wall next to the Stairmasters that blocked any view to the treadmill she was using. When I got to the corner of that wall, I rounded it, only to see her standing next to that treadmill, talking to one of her teammates. Not that I didn't have the guts to do it, but hitting on her in front of one of her friends was definitely a bad idea. That would be putting her on the spot. The first step I took toward her turned into the first step I took away, as I swiveled on my back foot and about-faced. I wonder if anyone saw. I probably looked ridiculous… I walked back out into the hallway and over to a PC there so I could check my e-mail (in order to waste some seconds so she could get herself over to the Stairmaster). After a few moments of scanning through the spam in my account, I closed the browser and walked back into the cardio room. She was there, standing on the Stairmaster and getting herself situated and ready to go. I took a quick breath in and walked up behind her, tapping her on the left shoulder. The moment of truth had come.

As soon as she turned to look at me, I was alright. Somehow, I focused and got to it. She looked a bit taken aback at first—as if she had never seen me before. I said hi and introduced myself. She introduced herself in return. (I won't divulge her name here, but we will call her "C" from this point on.) I already knew her name from looking her up online, but she didn't know that. I told her that I had seen her around the gym quite a bit and I was curious as to what she did. She understood what I meant and told me that she was on the school's gymnastics team. (Obviously, I knew that too.) After my response: "Oh. Well that explains it," she apologized to me because she had something in her eye and was still trying to get it out. I couldn't really tell because even though she thought her eye was "all red from rubbing at it," it matched the rest of her face. Unlike most people, C was actually in the habit of exerting herself at the gym. I loved that about her. I asked if I could get her some water, but she said she had just gotten some eye drops and was going to use them. Then, the conversation just sort of stopped. After a few seconds of silence, I told her that I wasn't going to beat around the bush. She giggled at that. That was a good sign, right? I told her that I had noticed her before and that I thought she was really attractive. C's reaction to that was puzzling to me. It actually looked like she had been hit in the face with an invisible two-by-four. She shook off the stun of it and thanked me. Her being rattled by that brought all my fears about the whole thing right back to life. I felt as though I might not be able to recover, but I went on. I asked her if she was single. To my great joy and relief, she said that she was, so I asked if I could take her out some time. Her response: "I don't know." It wasn't just a standard "I don't know," but one of those "I don't knows" where the "know" has two syllables: the first higher, the second lower in pitch. Was I wrong to believe that she was attracted to me? It sure seemed that way. Maybe she was playing hard-to-get. No matter. Whatever was going on, I had to figure out a way around it. I just kept being direct. "Why not?" I asked. She told me that she didn't know me. If I would have said what came to mind at that moment, it might have sounded condescending: "That's the whole point... That's what I'm trying to change." Instead of saying that, I looked down for a moment and let out a little laugh. Then I looked back up at her and said, "What do I gotta do to make that a yes?" She replied that I could call her. I responded to that with, "And you'll answer?" She told me she would. I got out my phone and recorded her number. I had done it—I got a foot in the door. It didn't feel like a victory though. I was pleased to get her number, but I had hoped it would be easier... nicer... I don't know. We made some small talk, and I told her that it was a pleasure to meet her. Afterwards, I started off towards home. I was relieved that I had finally talked to this woman, but I could see that I had a great distance to go before I arrived where I needed to be.

When DJ got home that evening, I told him what had happened. I had confided in him about the woman I had become smitten with recently, and he was glad to hear the news. Still, I was quick to point out that my victory didn't seem that much like one, so I wasn't celebrating just yet. I said all the standard, prudent things: "We'll just have to see how it goes"; "If it happens, it happens";

and the like. I was still trying to seem prudent, or nonchalant, or who knows what? In the face of my desire to stay under control, I could feel myself struggling to keep down a lot of things that were then starting to rise to the surface. I was having trouble accepting the intensity of my feelings for C, and I definitely didn't want DJ to know how overwhelmed I was starting to feel by it all. The truth is that I had begun having thoughts about C that I had no good reason to have, but no matter how I attempted to squelch them with logic and reason, my heart wouldn't have it. I feared that my feelings of isolation might be playing into the situation somehow, and I wondered sometimes if they were creating the entire infatuation. That just didn't make sense though. I had been so closed off to the idea of something like this happening just months before, yet there I was wide open and hoping. What if I got too wrapped up in it? I knew that my thinking patterns could become potentially destructive to my own psyche, especially if things didn't go the way I wanted them to. The last thing I wanted was to put myself at risk again, for fear that my heart might be damaged beyond repair. Yet the thoughts just came, and they continued to come. With more and more difficulty, I continued to say the prudent thing as I tried to keep myself grounded.

From the time I was a little boy, all the way through high school, the thing I wanted most was to be in love: to love someone and be loved in return. I spent so many nights lying in my bed and looking at the ceiling, wondering when my turn would come. I never could figure out how to actually date any of the girls I liked. I just didn't know what to say or do to win a girl over. Eventually, I begrudgingly fell in love with Mara. The reason for that was that she fell in love with me. She wasn't who I wanted at first, but I grew to love her for who she was. She was a wonderful person: kind and understanding. She had reached out for me when I desperately needed someone to—when my heart was reeling and I thought I might never get to love anyone. When our relationship faltered, as I have said before, I became jaded. I felt like love was an illusion. I had meant with all of my heart to marry her. For a time, we had something wonderful, but in the end, all I could do was watch as the romance we shared slipped out the back and vanished into the night. The time came, and I had no choice but to lay our tattered and torn love to rest. It died… despite how strong it had once been. I felt that we should have been able to keep it together, and I wondered how anyone could, if two devoted people like Mara and myself couldn't. But as time passed, I found it in my heart to care about her again and to forgive her for her part in it all. Forgiving her helped me to reconsider the whole idea of love, and I started to believe in it again. Eventually, the things I faced in Veiltown became overwhelming, and I became crushingly lonely. I started to need another heart to grasp onto. But this time, things would be different. I wouldn't make the mistakes I had made before. I would find the right woman, and I would give her everything she needed. She would never doubt how much she meant to me. I wouldn't allow myself to be petty or critical. No. That would happen when hell froze over. I would treat her like I should: like the most important thing in my life. I would be perfect... for her and for us. Somehow, though my faith had nearly been broken, and although I couldn't even fully admit it to myself, without much to base it on, something inside me was convinced that I had found the one. She was right there in front of me. All I had to do was figure out how to show her.

27

Par for the Course

School was getting closer and closer to its end. I couldn't wait. I was ready to be done with it all: the coursework, the clinic, the teachers, the building, the city, and especially the students. My plan had been to get up and out of Veiltown with as much haste as I could gather, as soon as school and the clinical board examination for licensure were over. Yet somehow, even with a mountain of pain and resentment to drive me out of town post haste, I was starting to consider the possibility of staying. Certain things would have to happen, but remaining in Veiltown after school had finished was no longer the most repulsive thought I could manufacture. No... There were now worse things to ponder, and my mind was busy working on finding ways to avoid them.

When I had spoken with her, C told me a little bit about her schedule and when I might be able to call her. She said the weekends would be the best time. I had every intention to wait until the weekend to call for the first time, but reality has a great way of leaving intentions unaccomplished. I was at the gym two days later. I had been fortunate enough to have my afternoon patient cancel, and I went in at around one-thirty PM, so I could get my workout in early and go home to take a nap.

At that point, instead of hoping to see C at the gym, I was hoping that I wouldn't. The first meeting between us had not helped me to become any less nervous about her. I wanted to wait a few days, calm down, and work out my nerves by talking to her on the phone. That would work well. It would be much easier than having to stand in her presence and struggle. If I had left the gym ten minutes earlier, I would have missed her. Damn… As I was walking out of the weight room on my way to the locker room, I noticed C working her abdominals in her favorite corner. I thought maybe she wouldn't see me for a second, but then our eyes met, right before she turned the opposite direction to focus on the other side of her core. I was stuck. I didn't want to hang around and wait for her to finish the set because I didn't want to become annoying. I just couldn't read how she was feeling at that point, so being overzealous was something I wanted to avoid. Besides that, I was still so nervous. But she saw me, and I didn't want to seem scared to talk to her because it would probably make me look timid. After a moment of consideration, I figured I should leave C to her work and I left. On the way home, I decided that I would call her—to acknowledge that I saw her and to say hi. I felt that I really didn't have a choice. I couldn't just act like it didn't happen.

Of all the phone conversations I've had in my life, that one may have been the worst. (There have been some bad ones too—mostly having to do with an outrageous medical bill I acquired because I tried to save a dog from getting hit by a car and, in the process, got bitten so hard that it chipped a bone. I would have rather had a couple of those conversations than the one I had with C that day.) You know how people communicate non-verbally with tone or body language? Well, C had a tone that stated very clearly that she didn't feel comfortable talking to me. When she answered, I identified myself and told her that I had seen her at the gym a few hours ago; I wanted to say hi because I didn't get a chance to there. She said she had noticed me. I asked her if she had some time to talk, and she hesitantly said that she did, so I asked her about her major and other such things. She said she was studying to become a teacher. I asked her about what classes she was taking, and she told me that she was taking a biology class where the teacher didn't like to harm living things, so they just watched plants and things grow. Had college actually become as exciting as "watching grass grow?" We hadn't talked for long when she suddenly said she had to go. I was really getting a bad vibe. It felt very much like she had an unfavorable perception of me, and I didn't enjoy that fact. I was a good guy. I wasn't some jerk to be suspicious about. Before we got off the phone, I told her that she didn't have to be shy around me. She said it was just because she didn't know me. I accepted that, wished her a pleasant evening, and told her that I would give her a call over the weekend. We said goodbye and the summary on my phone said that we had talked for a little over seven minutes. I just sat on my bed after that thinking. Why was it going so badly? Was it something I was doing? I only hoped that it would get better, and quickly.

Right around that time, I started to notice that I was having some minor issues with digestion. They were peculiar and sporadic. I figured they would go away on their own, but every time I thought I was in the clear, the problem would come back. During those episodes, my stomach experienced minor discomfort. It wasn't enough to interfere with my days, but it was definitely enough to concern me, especially given the fact that the episodes kept happening. I was focused on C though, so I just sort of put it to the side the best I could.

I should have guessed what would happen next. It isn't as if it was difficult to predict. I called C, and she responded poorly. Then she came up with an excuse to end the call after only a few minutes. Chances were that those things didn't bode well for me. Nevertheless, I intended to ride it out. True to my word, I called her that Sunday. I made sure that she didn't have a meet that day by looking at the team's online schedule (as I was accustomed to doing by that time). When I called in the afternoon, she didn't answer. I left a message and hoped that she would call back. She didn't, so I waited and waited some more. I wanted to call again, but I was patient and waited six days (until the next Saturday) before I did. No answer. I left another message.

I was becoming impatient and frustrated, so the next day, I called again after DJ and I had played Ultimate Frisbee with his friends from the economics program. As DJ drove us home, I pulled out my phone and dialed. Once again, C's recorded voice answered. I was getting ever so tired of her voicemail message. This time, I hung up and banged my head against the headrest a few times while letting out a progressively intensifying growl of sorts. DJ was on me in an instant. He wasn't happy about the way C was ignoring me. In his eyes, I was getting blown off. He felt that I should have a little bit more pride and just leave it be. "Why would you want to be with a woman like that anyhow? She isn't worth your time or effort." Of course, he probably saw better than I did just how affected I was at that point. Just as he should have been, he was trying to protect me. I was trying to give off the appearance that C wasn't intensely important to me, but she was. DJ knew it. He also knew that I was heading for a dangerous place. I either couldn't fully see it or just didn't care—I'm not sure which. Against DJ's admonitions that I should drop it and move on, I wasn't ready to give up just yet. I got him to ease up by telling him that he should know that no matter how clear something might look, it is never a good idea to make assumptions about what another person is feeling or going through. Notwithstanding his concern for me, he knew that I was right and accepted my decision to keep trying.

Why was this woman so important? Why would I be willing to keep going after all that? I was almost four years into a perfect storm, and the end was still far from sight. Nothing made sense. I was hollow: a shell of my former self. I couldn't do anything right. I had gradually become afraid to even talk to people because I was worried about saying the wrong thing and them looking down on me for it (just as I had been when I was a young boy). I thought I had left those days far behind, never to be revisited, and I hated my classmates for making me feel that way again. I had become so unsure of myself. How could I be sure of myself? If I could offend my best friends, how could I expect not to offend strangers? I found myself in a constant state of self-censorship. It seemed that being myself would only anger people, and that hurt more than I can explain. I don't think there can be many things that are more disheartening than when you absolutely love people and they hate you in return. Besides that, I was tired all the time. When my alarm would go off in the morning, it felt like the most terrible nightmare. I hated going to that building where all those people looked at me like I was a leper—where unfavorable opinions of me seemed to be bandied about as soon as my back was turned. Now, I had this digestive problem. I was still fighting all of it though. Only two people even had an idea of how deeply my wounds ran: DJ and Darren. I still tried hard to enjoy the life I had and to remember how blessed I was, but deep down inside, I was drowning. I had lost so many important things: love, direction, peace of mind, identity... I honestly didn't know who I was anymore. I was so mixed up that I could scarcely tell which way was up and which way was down. So when C came along, my heart latched right onto her. She was a beacon of light through an eternity of darkness. I couldn't tell anyone, but in her, all I could see was my salvation: a reason for those years of suffering and the reward at the end of a long, soul-depleting journey. After many nights pondering the matter, I had come to the conclusion that my feelings for her just couldn't be merely a product of my emotional troubles. No. She had something... something that resonated inside me in a way I had never felt. The harder it got with her, the more determined I became to make it work—somehow, some way. I had no choice but to exhaust every option I had.

28

A Shot in the Dark

Just to be safe, I waited a couple of days. C didn't call. What were my options then? I could wait until I saw her again at the gym and confront her. Does that sentence even sound like it would work? I didn't think so. Trying to explain complex feelings to someone in person is difficult at best, if not impossible. This is especially so if that person isn't willing to hear. Clearly I needed to communicate via a medium that would force C to process the things that were on my mind. As I had done with Paige, I decided to e-mail her. Did I have the right to do that? Maybe not, but doing so had gotten me somewhere with Paige, and there were some things I needed C to know. After I got her e-mail address from the student directory, I wrote her a rather long letter. I know that less is more for most people, but I had to make sure she understood where I was coming from. I wish I still had the letter. I kept it in my sent-mail folder for a long time, but I had to delete it, due to reasons that I will disclose later. I won't even try to reproduce it here, but I will give you the gist of it. I told C that I thought she had the wrong idea about me and that I didn't want to assume she wasn't interested because assumptions are often incorrect. Then, I painstakingly explained to her why I chose to hit on her and why I went about it the way I did (because it would have been transparent if I had tried to make small talk instead of just being up-front with my intentions). I told her that she was stunning. More importantly I told her that I could see that she wasn't typical or run-of-the-mill, and I was convinced that she was special. I told her that I really wanted to get to know her better, but if we spent some time and she wasn't interested, I would be fine with that. I asked her to get back to me, regardless of what she had to say, yes or no. I just didn't want to be ignored. I even told her that I had never been so nervous about talking to a woman, but I talked to her anyhow because I wasn't one to let fear control me. Maybe I shouldn't have been so honest, but I hoped that it would feel good to her to understand how she affected me. I sent the e-mail off with little hope that I would ever hear back from her, but little hope is better than none.

I sent the letter that Tuesday. I didn't really expect that C would reply, but there was at least some chance of it in my mind (or else I never would have sent the thing). One, two, three, four days passed. Nothing... She took all that sincerity and candor and discarded it, like a Christmas tree on New Year's Day. As a defense mechanism, I adopted DJ's stance on the situation: "Why would I want a girl who would blow me off?" I was like, "F her! I should have known not to talk to her. She's too young to understand. Whatever..." I was putting up a nasty little front. I wasn't really angry with C. How could I be? My mind just needed to protect itself from despair, so it used anger. I secretly held on to a progressively dwindling hope that she would write back. As each day passed, I started to accept it more and more. I was wrong about her. She wouldn't save me, even if she could. And really, why should she? I guess she just didn't think I was worth any of her time. I wished she would have written to say "no thanks," but so few people have the courage to actually confront these types of issues and be honest. I couldn't be mad at her for that. It wasn't her fault—more so a symptom of a larger societal problem.

If things would have continued on that way, my life would be very different now... very different. At that time, I could have let it go. I honestly would have too. My options were exhausted, and though I held onto the most miniscule bit of hope, I was starting to feel better. I think it was the definitiveness of the most recent events that helped me. I had a very clear answer; it was safe to say that C wasn't interested. I gave it my best, and I could be proud of that. Besides, I still wanted to get the hell out of Veiltown after graduation, and at that point, I didn't have to contemplate staying for C. How could I be happy if I had to stay in that place? Maybe it was for the best. On the bright side, I still had DJ and Darren. I hoped I could enjoy my time with them without having my mind constantly consumed by heavier things.

Ten days… Ten days after I sent C the letter, my last gasp at turning my situation around and winning her over, I had the fortune of a patient cancellation for my morning clinic session. I had some paperwork and other housekeeping duties to attend to, so I used the extra time to take care of them. I got done at about eleven AM and spent some time chatting with some of the faculty and my classmates. After that, at around noon, I made my way out of the building. It was Friday, and the sun was shining high in Veiltown's deep blue sky. The temperature was warm for that time of year too. In short, the day was glorious. I was excited to get out of the dental school and find a good way to waste the afternoon. After all I had gone through for the last month and a half, I needed a relaxing day. I was even whistling as I walked into the library to check my e-mail on the way off campus.

I can't honestly give you a reason why I checked the e-mail account that I had e-mailed C from that day. I seldom got anything but spam in that account, and I used two others much more frequently. I wasn't even thinking about it when I entered my username and password. I guess I had just gotten into the habit of checking it since I sent the letter. I don't remember thinking about her up to that point in the day. That was positive because for the last month and a half, I hadn't gone a few hours without her on my mind, much less half a day. I wouldn't make it ten more seconds. There, at the top of my inbox, was her name. After I processed it, it must have looked as if I had been hit in the face with something. I guess she was returning the favor. I stood there stunned for a moment, undesirable possibilities rampaging through my mind. I closed the browser and walked out the door just a few feet from the terminal I was at. I wasn't going to let her ruin my day—not that day. Maybe I would read it later. However, as I crossed the threshold of the doorway, the thought occurred to me: "Why would she wait so long to ruin my day? Why wouldn't she do it sooner?" Consequently, I turned right around and quickly stepped back to the PC I had just left. I opened my e-mail account and looked at C's name for a second. I closed my eyes momentarily, took a deep breath, opened my eyes again, and opened the letter. If anyone had watched my face as I read through it, they would have seen a progression from intensely focused, to slightly amused, to ecstatic. By the time I was finished, I was smiling as widely as my lips would allow, and there was nothing I could do to stop it. C told me that she was sorry for not responding earlier because she was busy being a student and an athlete. She did believe I was a nice guy, or else she wouldn't have given me her number. Unfortunately, she really didn't have time for "boys" at the moment because of gymnastics and school. (In my mind, I was like, "Boys? Girl, I'm a man!" That thought still makes me laugh.) After that, she said that when her season was over we might be able get to know each other better. It wasn't a green light, and I would have to wait a while, but it was an opening: an opportunity to go forward. I would have been thrilled with just that, but then there was the p.s. It read: "Thank you for the compliments… and to be honest, I noticed you at the gym as well." That p.s. turned out to be the cause of the most exhausted set of facial muscles that anyone must have ever had. I just couldn't stop smiling. I'm sure I must have looked like the most blissful idiot. I got on the bus and just smiled away. In every conceivable way, it was a perfect day. Finally! Something good had happened to me. It was about time.

When DJ got home at around three PM, I was happily singing along with one of my R&B CD's and washing dishes after my afternoon meal. DJ walked into the kitchen and looked at me. He just stared for a moment with a perplexed look on his face. I don't think he had seen me that happy in years. I could see in his expression that he had an idea what had happened, but he asked anyhow. I laughed as I told him that C had written back and that her reply was positive. DJ was happy for me. I hurried him into my room and pulled up the e-mail on my computer. He read through it quickly, and then turned to me with a solemn look and said, "Well... now you've got what you wanted." I did have what I wanted. I did! I could scarcely believe it, and I definitely couldn't contain my excitement. By the time I went to bed that night, my face was in pain from half a day of the most unexpected happiness. Even so, I was still smiling when I fell asleep.

29

Free Fall

At that point, the gymnastics season was going to take at least a month and a half to finish. Although I wanted to get to spending time with C as soon as possible, I didn't want her season to be over that quickly. I hoped it would go longer. After the conference championships, it was the norm for the team to go on to regionals. Then, if they placed high enough there, they could go to nationals and compete for the NCAA championship. Sadly, the team wasn't doing so hot at that point in the season. I hoped it would turn around for them (and especially for C). I know first hand that athletes live to compete and to win. Losing sucks, and there is no worse feeling than knowing that you could have done better. I was hoping that it would take about two months before C and I would have some time to start working things out.

It took me a couple of days to respond to C's message. I didn't want to seem too excited about her reply. Isn't dating complicated? Man! Don't show your hand too soon. When I did write back, I attempted to be as understanding and kind as I possibly could. Obviously, I didn't want to distract her from what she was focused on. Whatever she wanted to do was fine with me. I was happy to wait for her season to be over. I told her to just let me know what she wanted to do and when. When I finished the letter, I was feeling just a bit cocky and I wanted to flirt a little, so I wrote her a p.s. of my own. My p.s. read: "Your p.s. made me smile, and I'm glad that you told me that… but to be honest, I already knew." (Then I left a little winking smiley face.) I still don't know whether that was a mistake or not.

I went about my normal daily routine, but with a bit more vigor. At some point in my life, I had become familiar with a quote that I felt was particularly poignant. I don't know who first said it, but the quote states, "Happiness is having something to look forward to." With a future that included a date with C, I couldn't have agreed more because I was so very happy. It had been about four days since I had sent my flirtatious response, and I was at the gym on a Sunday afternoon. I had finished my weight routine, and I was walking up the stairs to the ground floor when around the corner came the most incredible thing: five feet three inches tall, lean and muscular, with bleached blonde hair in a high pony tail and a rose-tinted patch of brown below it, deep blue eyes, a face covered with the most gorgeous freckles, every inch and every curve on her body so, so right… I could feel myself getting nervous once again, but it wasn't paralyzing or distressing like before. It was intoxicating; she was intoxicating. I liked the feeling ever so much. C said hi as soon as she saw me. Then she stopped on the steps next to me. I smiled and said "Hey," in return. With greetings out of the way, we had a little chat. She talked so quickly as she explained to me how she had injured her knee and had to take it easy for a while. She also had to wear this funny bandage that was supposed to help with swelling by draining lymphatic fluid from the area. The bandage looked like some sort of octopus that wrapped around her thigh and calf. She could make anything look sexy. I listened and nodded and didn't say much. I wanted to talk, but I was too mesmerized. The way she rambled was adorable. It seemed for all the world that she was actually nervous, and that filled me with the most incredible sense of hope. When we parted, she asked me if I was just starting. I told her that I was about finished and that I would be leaving soon. She told me she would be upstairs on an elliptical rider because she wasn't allowed to run. I reached out for her hand, and when she gave it to me, I squeezed it and told her that it was good to see her. She returned the sentiment and we parted ways.

In retrospect, I was the biggest fool that day. I should have gone upstairs and talked more with her. I should have taken the opportunity to show her a little more about who I was and how I conducted myself—to get comfortable around her and to let her get comfortable around me. Regretfully, I was trying to play "the game." I felt that I shouldn't seem too interested. I didn't even think about the fact that the way I had conducted myself had already committed me to being interested. I'm sure that acting like I had more important things to do than take every opportunity to know her was clearly a front, and it made me look bad. Nonetheless, I was oblivious to what I had just done.

I had only mentioned C in passing to Darren: "There is this girl at the gym I have been thinking about talking to," and such. He had no clue how infatuated I really was. That day was the day I was going to tell him. After leaving the gym, I excitedly jumped in my car and started driving to his house, once again smiling like a buffoon. I called to tell him I was on my way there and asked if he wanted to go grab some burritos. He was down. When I got to his house, I was about to burst. Darren let me in and, well, I did! First, I asked him if he remembered the girl I had told him about from the gym, and he did. I went into detail about what I had gone through over the past month and a half as I attempted to communicate with her. I told him about the letter I had written after C had not returned my phone calls and how she had finally written back on Friday. Then I told him what had just happened. Darren listened politely, quietly analyzing what I said.

After I finished my story, some words that I didn't see coming just sort of popped out. "Dogg, I'm going to marry this woman." WHAT? Did I really mean that? Was I really that foolish? Did I honestly think that I could tell enough about her at that point that I was willing to predict spending the rest of my life with her? Well I said it, so I must have. Now Darren looked like HE had been hit in the face by something. He stared at me—just as stunned as could be—and said, "Really?! Wow…" In that moment, I had completely come to grips with what all of it actually meant: everything. I got on Darren's computer and showed him the e-mail I had sent to C. After he read the letter, he looked somewhat taken aback. He opened his eyes wide, shook his head a bit, and asked, "Isn't that a bit intense?" I felt somewhat indignant at his response, but I was so overwhelmed with anticipation of things to come that I just smiled and said, "It worked didn't it? Look at her reply." After he read that, he said, "Okay… If it worked, it worked. Just don't get ahead of yourself man. I don't want to see you get hurt." What a good friend. But there was no way I was going to think rationally about it; I wasn't capable. Nothing in the world could have pulled me back at that point. All my chips were in. I was betting the house, the car, and the family dog.

30

The Wait

A couple of days passed, and I started to think that I really wanted to see C compete before the season was over. The team had one more home gym meet before a string of road meets at the end of the season, and I wanted to go. I sent C an e-mail asking if she wouldn't mind if I came to "one of her home meets" to watch. (I was still trying to hide the fact that I was keeping track of her progress.) I told her that if she didn't want me to, it was no big deal; I didn't want to distract her. I expected that she would reply, but days went by, and the meet passed without a word from her. That filled me with doubt. Had I done something wrong when we last saw each other? I decided that I shouldn't dwell on it, because I was tired of worrying and didn't want to go back to it. Regardless, the fact sat in a corner of my mind and festered.

During the next couple of months, I tried to keep my mind on other things. I was a bit behind on my requirements at school, and I needed to hustle if I was going to get them all done in the next quarter and a half before graduation. I scheduled patients when I had open clinic sessions, and slowly but surely, things began to come together. As the days went by, I kept an eye on the gymnastics team's results. Every time C had a bad performance, I suffered. Every time she did well, my spirits picked up. I truly hoped her season would extend itself as far as possible; it didn't matter that I would have to wait even longer if that were the case. There was no thought in my mind of competing with C's hopes and dreams; I would gladly take a backseat to them. Truly, whatever would make her happy was what I wanted. I talked with Darren and DJ about the whole situation often, trying to get their insights. I didn't want to seem like a cretin, so I kept saying the logical and levelheaded thing. Clearly, they both knew that I was putting up a front. It speaks greatly to their characters that they were supportive in spite of any reservations they had. They both understood me well enough to know that being negative or critical wouldn't change anything. The way I felt about C was written all over my face. It echoed in my voice and followed me around like my own shadow. There was no shaking it.

Before I met C, I had begun taking private ballroom dance lessons every week. After a few weeks, I had invited Kristina to be my partner and come to my lessons with me. We would go to lessons on Sundays, and then we would push the furniture out of my living room and practice what we had learned on Thursday nights. While I was with Mara, I had been somewhat against dancing. Before I met her, I liked to dance. Regrettably, early in our relationship, she told me that she didn't "like the way I moved." It was a biting insult, and I sort of brooded over it for the rest of our time together. After that comment, if she wanted to go dancing, I would try to come up with an excuse. We went occasionally, and sometimes I had a good time, but it was always in the back of my mind that Mara was criticizing my skills. Typical of any human (especially a male), criticism from a loved one damaged my pride. Since Mara and I had broken up, I liked to dance again and I had done a good bit of it at the clubs with Darren. That was just random hip-hop dancing though, and I wanted more, so I began taking ballroom lessons. Kristina and I had great fun each week attending our lesson and then practicing our new moves at my home. I'd say we got relatively good rather quickly. We moved through the basics and a little extra on

The Wait

one-step, foxtrot, swing, and merengue. While I was waiting for C's season to finish, we were working on swing. I loved dancing with Kristina, but we were just good friends by that point. Whenever we danced, I imagined doing it with C. She would be perfect as a dance partner because she was just the right size, as well as more agile and athletic than any woman I was likely to meet. I couldn't help but fantasize about flipping her into the air or spinning her around in quick, tight circles or just being close to her as we moved to the rhythm. I would mean so much to me. After we finished practicing and Kristina had gone home, I would lie in bed and dance with C in my mind until I fell asleep.

The conference championships came and went. Sadly, C's team missed regionals for the first time ever. They just had too many injuries to compete at their normal level. Nevertheless, C made it to regionals as an individual competitor in the all-around. I would have to wait at least a little while longer. I didn't mind at all.

I hadn't seen C since the day we last spoke, and I wasn't expecting that I wouldn't again before she finished. One day, I was at the gym with Darren. He and I had started lifting together at the beginning of the quarter, which was to be my last in dental school. It was good to have a partner again. It helped keep me motivated in my constant state of fatigue. We would lift hard and carry on like high schoolers: jokes, jokes, jokes nonstop. After I finished a set of incline bench press and Darren was about to start, I glanced over towards the entrance to the room. There was C, talking to her twin friends. "Dammit," I thought. I would have to go say hi. I didn't want to talk to her that day, but if she saw me and I didn't come greet her, once again, I felt it would make me look timid. I walked over to say hi while Darren waited by our bench. When I got close, one of the twins noticed me passing close to her, and her face showed a somewhat startled expression. (It was kind of funny.) I sort of snaked my way through the two of them and greeted C. I should have introduced myself to her friends, but guess what: I was really nervous again. Go figure. I think the length of time since our last conversation really made it hard for me that day. She didn't seem nervous though—rather more like she wanted to get me out of her hair as soon as possible; and I stuttered and repeated myself and just flat-out floundered. Smooth… I can't help but think that maybe her friends had some not-so-favorable things to say regarding me after that. I wouldn't be upset at them for it if it turned out to be true. I mean, I acted like a colossal dork! I knew it immediately. But it was done. It bugged me for the rest of the night and for a while afterwards, but I couldn't undo it; I just had to overcome it.

After that, I noticed that my digestion was acting up again. I still figured that it was only a temporary thing, but I had to acknowledge the fact that I had been having the problem for a pretty long while. Being consumed with something I deemed more important, I again pushed it aside (although I was a bit more concerned at that point). I hoped it would just work itself out.

The Thursday before the regional meet, I went to the gym. The meet was on Saturday, and C and a teammate of hers (who had also qualified as an individual competitor) were doing cardio when I arrived. Still gun-shy from talking to her a few days previously and also not wanting to break her focus in any way before the meet, I just tried to stay hidden from her view. I'm sure she saw me, but we never said anything to each other. I didn't want to make any more mistakes, so deciding not to talk to her was somewhat of a relief. Anyhow, in two days I would know when the season would be over. It would either be that day or two weeks later, and I was more than ready to stop wondering.

When the regional meet came, C did just fine, but not good enough to make it to nationals. Her season was over. I was really hoping she would take the initiative to give me a call or an e-mail and set up a time for us to meet. If you have read between the lines up to this point, you can be pretty safe in making a prediction that it didn't happen. I waited until mid-week and called her. I left a message saying that I had "noticed" in the paper that her season was over and that I was hoping she would have some time to get together with me soon. Again, days passed with no response. By the next week, my insecurities and damaged self-esteem had me figuring that C was going to blow me off again. I did have some other hypotheses about what was going on though. Since she had been consumed by her duties as a collegiate gymnast from December on through the previous week, including spring break, I thought that it was possible that she might have gone back home for a few days, to see her family and recover a little sanity. I also knew that she couldn't be gone for too long. Few people can pass college courses if they miss large chunks of time. The classes usually move too quickly to catch up without exerting a colossal effort (and the instructors are often less than accommodating).

By Tuesday of the next week, I couldn't keep myself from calling C again. I had a rough morning in clinic, which put me in a poor state of mind. I decided to walk through main campus to go to the gym in the ridiculously unlikely hope that I would see her walking. It was a nice day and all, and she didn't have so much to do anymore, so why wouldn't she be out enjoying the sunshine? Predictably, I didn't see her. I didn't see her at the gym either. It was around three-thirty PM by the time I got home, and I had had it. "Screw it!" I thought. "I don't care if I'm being pushy. Anything will be better than waiting and wondering this way! If I mess it up by calling again, oh freaking well." (Obviously, I didn't really mean that last part, but I took the chance and called anyhow.) To my surprise, for the first time since I had first dialed her number nearly three months before, C's voice rang out from the other end of the line.

Gathering myself quickly, I said hi and identified myself. She quickly asked if I could call her back in about five minutes. I was fine with that, so we hung up and I waited the five minutes. When I called back, she answered quickly and apologized. She told me how she was about to speak to her advisor before I called because she was going to attend summer school. We chatted a bit, and it was pleasant. She didn't seem annoyed or anything like that—just really nice and easy to talk to. That calmed my nerves quite a bit, making it much less difficult for me to just be easy and sincere. She told me she had gotten my voicemail, but hadn't called because she took off for home to visit her family after regionals. It was just as I had hoped. We talked for a few minutes about normal stuff, such as her plans after college. Along with being a teacher, she also wanted to compete in fitness competitions. I was thrilled to hear that. I had wondered if she would keep herself in great shape after her college athletic career ended, and she had just answered that question in the absolute best way I could think of. (I had always had a thing for fitness girls.) C expressed some concern that it would be hard to get in that good of shape, but also that she would enjoy the challenge. I was quick to point out that I felt she could compete in those things right then. She disagreed, but thanked me for saying so. Not wanting to take up her time, I decided to ask when we could get together. In response, she asked me what I was doing the coming weekend. I had anticipated it being hard for me to actually get her to come out, so I was elated to hear that she wanted to do it soon. I told her that I didn't have any plans, so whatever worked for her would work for me. She said she was going to be working for a friend in the fitness industry at a show that weekend, basically representing his company at a booth. She would be working that Friday and Saturday evening, but she was free Sunday in the day. I offered to take her to lunch, and she agreed to meet me. I wasn't sure exactly where I wanted to take her, so I asked her if I could call her later in the week with a proposal. She said that I could. I thanked her and we said goodbye. The roller coaster was back on the upswing, and not a moment too soon. I had been having real difficulty sleeping for a few weeks, and my stomach had been killing me. That conversation was like a week's vacation. I was instantly refreshed. I went to bed at around nine PM that evening, and I fell asleep within seconds. I slept straight through the night. That week, I don't recall even thinking about my digestion.

That week was as busy as could be. I was swamped with clinic sessions at school, but I was floating, so no amount of patient care drama could dampen my spirits. This thing was going to work out. Finally, I would have something to show for what I had been through. When I thought about all I had endured, just regarding C, I strangely almost felt like it had been easy: like I could go through it one hundred more times—one million more times even—if the end result would be me getting close to her. (It was absolutely gut-wrenching in reality.) On Friday, I had figured out where I wanted to take her, and when I finished with my afternoon patient, I planned to call C on my way to an ultimate Frisbee league game I was going to play in. My afternoon appointment ran long though, and I wasn't finished until an hour and a half after clinic normally ended. (My supervisor had stayed with me while I worked on an ultimately doomed upper denture with a metal plate in the palate area.) There was no way I would make it to the game, but that didn't really matter to me.

Before I started cleaning up the unit I had been in, I stepped outside onto the balcony overlooking the lake behind the school and called C. I told her that I wanted to take her to a Mexican restaurant downtown. Unbeknownst to her, I knew a lot about her from looking at her online biography. One of the things I knew was that her favorite type of food was Mexican. Ergo, I should take her to get Mexican. She agreed to it. Great! I also mentioned that I wanted to take her to a certain park in the area. The park had a beautiful scenic view of downtown and the waterfront. She wasn't sure if she would be able to, but she said we could play it by ear. We talked for a few more minutes about the weekend and such. It was an even better conversation than the last one. Before we got off the phone, we agreed to meet on Sunday at noon at a Mexican restaurant on the top floor of one of the malls downtown. The last thing I said before we said goodbye was, "I'm looking forward to it." In return C said, "Yeah... me too." I stood on the balcony and looked at the water for a few minutes after the conversation ended. There I was. I was so sure that it was going to happen that I could taste it. I WAS going to marry her. (She just didn't know it yet.) My soul was set ablaze with this amazing feeling... I couldn't wait to show C what I had for her, and it was just a matter of time.

31

Paradise Lost

If I named the important days in my life, the day of my date with C would now be labeled "Black Sunday." Never have I had such a high turn into such a low. What was worse was how quickly it happened. I was so optimistic about our meeting. I arrived downtown early and walked around the city streets for about an hour. The morning sun was bright and the air was crisp and clear. It was an encouraging setting for a first date. Soon discovering I was hungry, I tried a tuna salad at a little café, but couldn't get it down because I was so jittery. I guessed I would have to wait until C and I met up at the restaurant. I had really wanted to get C a gift of some sort: something sweet that would give her some insight into me. The night before, I had decided I would give her a white rose. A white rose stands for honesty, so I thought it would be a nice gesture. I picked one up at an open-air market in the area and headed back to the mall. When I got there, I still had thirty minutes, so I went to the restaurant and had the hostess put the rose on a table I picked for us to sit in. Afterwards, I went to Macy's and looked around for a bit. While I was there, I ran into Jenny and Will, a couple I knew from school. The two of them had graduated, one and two years before me, respectively. They were both real cool, and I had run into them in a couple of other places before. Neither of them had seen me since my surgery, and they were both very complimentary about the results. I had just gotten my braces off that week too. Jenny said I looked "great." I was happy to hear that, being as I was about to go on the most important date of my life. Any little boost in confidence would help. It had been good to see them both, but I had to go. It was about that time.

When I stepped off the elevator on the top floor, in the distance, I could see C standing in front of the restaurant waiting. I could pick her out at any distance. She was wearing a pair of blue jeans and a frilly black shirt with black high heels. As I walked over to meet her, I took her in. She had sparkles on her chest and neck, and her eyes were like searing blue flames. It was the first time I had ever seen her in makeup, or regular clothing for that matter. What more can I say than that she looked amazing? She said hi to me as I came within speaking range. I smiled and said, "You never disappoint, do you?" First bad omen: she didn't hear what I said; I could tell by her response. Besides that, she had an unconcerned vibe about her. I hoped it was just something I could work through. I was about to find out.

When we got to the table, she didn't seem very thankful for the rose that was waiting there for her. "Damn!" What was going on? It wasn't supposed to happen that way. Ever the optimist, I convinced myself that I could recover as we took our seats and began to look at the menus. The entirety of the forty-five minutes we spent together doesn't need to be recounted here, but I will give you a summary. One positive was that she talked a lot. That was a wonderful thing in my opinion. I needed a woman with a strong, assertive personality, because mine can be overwhelming sometimes. I had decided not to speak a whole lot that day because of my lackluster history on first dates in Veiltown. I didn't want to be too verbose, too honest, or just too much. (But C wasn't from Veiltown… Had I forgotten?) She filled the silence just fine without much help from me. I had no problem with that. It was more her lack of eye contact and warmth that shook me. She was just so distant and cold. Another problem revealed itself in some of the questions she asked. First, she asked me how old I was. I had already told her that in my letter, but I answered anyhow. It seemed that our age difference was somehow a problem as she told me in response that she was twenty-one. I was convinced that it was a non-issue and that if she couldn't see that yet, she would in time. Besides that, she told me she traveled to my hometown for a couple of days when she visited her own home after regionals. I asked, "How did my hometown treat you?" Later on in the conversation, she asked me where I was from. Was she joking? I had told her three times to that point: once the first time we spoke, once in the letter I sent her, and once more just four minutes prior. I sort of let on that I was a bit offended by her lack of attentiveness. My delusions were crumbling like so many Butterfinger candy bars crammed into a cowboy's pocket, but I was holding onto them tenaciously. So what if she didn't remember some things? She had been really busy and probably had a lot on her mind. It was a forgivable offense. Next she lied to me. I asked if she had gotten my letter asking her if I could come to one of her home meets. She said she had, but at that point, the team didn't have any more home meets left on the schedule, so she didn't write back. Even if that were true, she could have written back. It was a lame excuse, but people lie about those sorts of things all the time, so I still wasn't ready to be angry at her. Then there were the stupid things I said. Even while barely speaking, I managed to blurt out some stuff that I just should have kept to myself, at least until she knew me better. But no matter how much I wanted to, I couldn't take it back.

Only thirty minutes in, she told me that she had to be back to campus to meet up with some classmates for a study session by one-fifteen PM. She needed to leave in fifteen minutes. I couldn't believe that she had only planned to give me forty-five minutes. How could we even start to get to know each other in such a small amount of time? Was that all I deserved? I asked her if we could possibly go to the overlook, but she seemed really hesitant to even try it—didn't think she had enough time. I was rapidly nearing the bitter end of a long and tortuous

journey. I suggested, "Maybe another time… provided we go on another date."
All I can do to even make an attempt at explaining what happened then is to say
that I don't so much remember the way they sounded, but I still FEEL the words
she spoke next: "I don't know." The same "I don't know" from the day we met. If
I had been standing, I think my legs would have buckled underneath me. As it
was, it took every bit of self-control I possessed to block the most overwhelming
urge that immediately welled up inside of me: the urge to burst into tears. And I
mean I just barely kept it together. I was only a split second away from getting up
to go to the bathroom so she wouldn't see me cry. The muscles in my legs
actually twitched to start the standing motion, but I changed my mind and sat
through it. Nonetheless, I was so leveled that all I could muster in return was a
weak and conceding "C'mon." She had never intended to give me a chance.
Suddenly, her willingness to go out with me so quickly made an unfortunate
variety of sense: she just wanted to get it out of the way so she could be done
with me, but also so she could say that she "gave me a chance." After a few more
moments at the table, we got up to leave. I walked with her to the elevator and
we made some small talk. I can't for the life of me recall what was said though,
because I was long gone. When we got to the elevator, she hugged me before she
got on. I had long anticipated the day that I could put my arms around her and
pull her close, but I don't remember how the hug felt. I'm not even sure that I felt
it at all. I just remember the most intense and incapacitating pain.

Once she left, I don't know how I kept myself from crying for so long.
My natural defense mechanisms (anger, pride, etc.) must have somehow slowed
my descent. I staggered down to street level and made it to my car; then I drove
straight to the overlook, parked, and walked over to the railing. Once there, I
stared forlornly at the water for, oh, half an hour. I can't remember the sound of
the people walking by or the smell of the air or the touch of the breeze on my
face. For thirty minutes, it was as if I just left the world. Eventually, my phone
started to vibrate in my pocket and I answered it. It was DJ. He's such a good
friend… I could tell he was excited for me and anticipating something good.

Me: "Hey man."

DJ: "Well?"

Me: "Well…"

DJ: "How did it go?"

As soon as he asked that and I had to think about the date directly, I was done for. My eyes filled right to the top with tears—so many that I lost any functional ability to see. Though I wanted to, I couldn't choke back the anguish in my voice as I tried to reply.

Me: "… … … Terrible."

DJ: "NO! Really?!"

Me: "Yeah…"

DJ: "What the hell happened?"

Me: "She barely looked at me… Didn't pay any attention to what I had to say… Fuck…"

True to form, DJ did his best to convince me that I couldn't make any evaluation about the date yet. He suggested that C was probably nervous. There had to be a logical explanation. But even DJ's positivity couldn't win against the truth of the day: C made it clear to me right there at that table that there would be no second date.

After about twenty minutes on the phone, I let DJ go. I stayed a little while longer at the overlook, lamenting that such a beautiful day had been forever destroyed in my memory. I had gotten plenty of sleep the night before, but as I got into my car, a wave of exhaustion hit me hard. When I got home twenty minutes later, I went straight into my room and collapsed on the bed. My dogs both jumped up to lie next to me. I wasn't in the habit of letting them sleep on my bed with me, but at the moment, I was too out of it to kick them off. Besides, they made me feel just the slightest bit better. I slept from around three PM until the late evening.

When I awoke, I decided that I should write C an e-mail and thank her for the date. It was the polite thing to do. (In my heart, I knew that she was through with me, but well, hope springs eternal.) I quickly typed out a message and sent it off. It was only a few lines. I thanked C for coming out and told her that I had a good time (even though that was far from true). Then I mentioned that I had forgotten to tell her (because I was pretty taken aback by her response to the thing) that a white rose stands for honesty. The study session she had left our date to attend was for some tests that week, so I wished her luck on them and said goodbye. I know what I expected back from her, but in retrospect, I wasn't ready to read it when it actually came. At any rate, I didn't get much rest that night because I had just finished a short night's sleep. Besides that, it was impossible not to dwell on the events of the day.

I was more exhausted than usual when morning came, as I dragged myself to school and saw my morning patient. The appointment extended into lunchtime, and I had just enough time to get a snack and go to the library to check my e-mail. C had written back the night before. As I read the blow-off letter, my sadness rapidly transformed into rage. I was deeply wounded, and as we all know, wounded animals fight fiercely. She told me that she couldn't see us ever being more than friends and that our age difference put us at "different points in our lives." I didn't have time to reply because I had to go extract teeth in my oral surgery clinic rotation, but she was going to get it. I had a whole bag of ammunition for her, and I didn't intend to stop firing until the end of the gun was melting. I remembered how I had told C in my first letter to her that I would be okay with it if we didn't click. So much for that... At that moment, a rare thing happened to me: I let a moment of anguish and anger shape my thoughts and actions for months to come. The outcome would not be productive.

I had noticed a very attractive woman sitting at a PC on the way into the room I was in. Now that I was free of all that nonsense I was stupid enough to feel for C, I could do something about it. I had not hit on another woman since the day I decided that I was going to talk to C, but that was about to change. I walked right over to the woman and told her she was gorgeous. She responded the way a woman should respond to a compliment: she smiled and thanked me sincerely. We introduced ourselves, and I asked her how old she was (because I was through talking to immature twenty-one year olds). I was pleased to find that she was twenty-four. Much better. I asked if she was single. She was married. Oh well. There were plenty of other women out there. Why would anyone think that there was only one who would work? I smiled and told her that her husband must be an impressive fellow. I wished her a good day, and I went on my way.

All I could think about during oral surgery was what I was going to say in my letter to C. Luckily for me, I was assigned to assist a classmate on an extraction that day. In the state of mind I was in, I don't think I would have wanted me as the primary caregiver. I might have removed someone's whole jaw. When I got home in the evening, I went straight for my computer and let loose. I was proper and cordial, but also brutally honest. I told C that I didn't appreciate her giving me lip service. I told her that I thought it was rude of her to pay so little attention to what I said to her. I told her that she was cold and distant. I told her that she had made a very poor impression on me. However, I also told her that I wasn't ready to write her off just yet, because in my experience, you couldn't tell much about a person from a forty-five minute date and a few short phone conversations; people were far too complex for that. (If you'll remember, I basically told Paige the same thing, only in a nicer way.) I also expressed that I couldn't predict the future, but I knew for sure that I couldn't somehow foresee what might happen between us if we actually got to know each other. I told her that if our age difference was a problem, she shouldn't have agreed to come out with me; I had told her how old I was in my first letter. I would have accepted a "No thank you, our age difference is too much." (Just one of the many ironies of this is that SHE was concerned with our age difference. What?) The tone of the letter was just flat-out mean. No, I didn't call her names, but I insulted the hell out of her actions, and I very clearly insinuated that she was naïve. At the end of the letter, I had the nerve to tell her that I didn't have anything against her and that I wished her luck and happiness in the future. I ended with a p.s. that informed her of how I was aware that she lied to me about my request to come to one of her home meets—I had looked at the schedule after I asked her. It's funny how I expected C to tell me the truth when I couldn't do the same. And to think, acting like a child and lashing out at her actually made me feel better. (At least I thought it did.)

32

Rebound

I don't know how, but after I sent the letter off, I was okay. I had work to do, so I didn't have time to feel sorry for myself. C was the one who missed out, not me. As it turned out, my initial appraisal of the situation had been correct: C was too young for me to date. She wouldn't know how to appreciate me anyhow. Darren and DJ were quick to support me in my wounded condition, and their kindness was welcome. With my pride smarting and up in arms, I buckled down and got to my duties. I sure as hell didn't want to have to stay another quarter to complete unfinished requirements. Then there was the clinical board examination for licensure. I still had to figure out how to get some patients for that. No matter. I would take care of it.

Things went pretty smoothly for a while. Darren and I continued to lift weights at the gym and we hung out whenever we could. He went through quite a few of his own trying times during the two years since we had met, and leaning on each other had brought us close. We knew all about each other's trials and tribulations, and we spent a good deal of time just mulling things over. DJ was there as well, always positive and willing to lend an ear. After a month or so, I even started dating again. I met a cute little lady named Karen on the bus one day, and we ended up getting together. She was intelligent, spunky, and fun, and I enjoyed her company quite a bit. Interestingly enough, she was only twenty years old. Regardless, I felt that she was very mature; plus, she had been assertive in talking to me, so I just went with it. I also started looking into work opportunities in the Los Angeles area. I wanted to live near the ocean and in a sunnier climate, so LA seemed ideal. I was looking forward to getting out of Veiltown and starting my real life. I had been in school for so many years, and I was happily anticipating the feeling of finally being free of ridiculously early lectures, homework, tests, and clinical requirements.

The first day I had gone back to the gym after my surgery, I was running around the track upstairs and I noticed Paige running on a treadmill. I didn't think she saw me Even if she did, I figured she might not have recognized me because my face was still a bit swollen. At any rate, I started thinking about my interactions with her; they still bugged me, only in different ways. One of the things she had told me on our date was that her father was very ill and had recently been admitted to the hospital. Time had given me some perspective on the whole situation and, as I am likely to do, I felt remorseful. It seemed to me that I hadn't really taken into account how Paige might have been feeling about the things that were going on in her life at the time. I didn't want to pressure her, but I had been lonely and pressing to find "Miss Right." My focus on that aspect of my life had put me in blinders and made me oblivious to much of what was going on around me. I wanted to apologize, so I e-mailed her, explaining exactly what I have just related here. I felt terrible about how I had acted, and I figured that even if Paige didn't want to be my friend, she would appreciate a heartfelt apology. After I sent the letter, she never had written back.

Darren and I were in the gym lobby one afternoon and Paige walked right past us. When I saw her, I didn't really think about it and just blurted out her name. She stood perplexed for a second, but her face soon showed recognition and she greeted me, even using my name. That was a good sign. I introduced her to Darren, and we stood and talked for a moment. As it turned out, she had decided that she wanted to move to Los Angeles in the next few months. "Great!" I thought. That would give us an opportunity to develop a friendship. That was all I really wanted—just to make things right between us. I was quick to inform her that I was also heading that direction as soon as I finished school. In all, our conversation lasted about three or four minutes. When we parted, I felt a little better about everything that had gone on before. Perhaps she had read the letter and decided to forgive me. I didn't mention keeping in touch with her, but I hoped we would run into each other again.

Little victories aside, one major problem continued: my digestion kept getting worse. It had been four months since I first noticed any symptoms, and despite my efforts to ignore them, they just wouldn't and didn't clear up. I was getting rather distressed, and I couldn't put it off any longer. I needed to see a doctor.

When Mara and I broke up, we made a decision that I would keep the dogs for a year and Mara would take them off my hands when she graduated and got situated. After finishing school, Mara had left Veiltown and, in her transition state, couldn't handle the responsibility of pets. I ended up keeping the boys for two years total. It was extremely difficult to get them the proper exercise with my ridiculous school schedule, exercise routine, and lack of sleep. I tried, but sometimes I couldn't find the time to walk them. Somehow, I kept the two of them healthy and safe until it was time for Mara to take them. Near the end of my last quarter in dental school, I was to meet Mara and her new boyfriend across state lines so that I could hand off the pups.

The night before we were to travel, Rusty had an accident in the house: a huge, watery, pungent, disgusting accident. It was the kind of accident all dog owners fear. DJ and I had been out at the movies, and when we walked into the house, ready to snooze, we had run into a wall of fumes coming from the kitchen. Cleaning up the mess was the most wonderfully nauseating experience. There was sooo much of it! On top of that, all I wanted to do was sleep. As I finished the task, I had the thought that maybe I had been carrying around a parasite that I had gotten from one of my dogs. I mean, it was possible that Rusty had been having sub-clinical symptoms for the last few months, and I just didn't notice. It wasn't like I had been examining his poop with a magnifying glass, looking for abnormalities. I was convinced that I had figured out the cause of my problem. I would tell Mara about Rusty's issues, and she could take him to the vet. As for me, I had an appointment at the campus health center the next week, and I was certain that they would tell me I had a parasite and then give me the proper antibiotics, thus ending four months of digestive unrest.

The next day passed, taking my dogs with it. Rusty started dancing frantically in the backseat about halfway to the rendezvous point, and luckily, I deduced why just in time to get the car stopped and him out of it before he unloaded a steaming, bloody pile. I was concerned about the blood, but I would get him to Mara and she would take care of it. She always did. I was sad to let my boys go, even though I knew it was for the best. There was no way I could keep them in Los Angeles with me while I figured out a job and living arrangements. I got a little choked up on my way home, but I have always slept easily knowing that Percival and Rusty are safe, happy, and healthy with Mara.

When my doctor's appointment came, I was more than ready to get my problem fixed. It had been dragging on for too long. First, I visited the lab and had blood drawn. I really hate having blood drawn. Needles in my mouth and shots into muscles, I can handle; but when they stick that huge, hollow-bore needle into the big vein that runs over the inside of my elbow joint, every muscle in my body tenses and I sit there waiting breathlessly for the moment when they pull it out. That day was no exception. It sucked (like usual) but it had to be done. Then I had to give the lab a stool sample and a urine sample. Urine samples are easy; stool samples are disgusting. I won't go into detail on this, but I sincerely hope that you yourself never have to give one. As I went through the process of actually getting the "sample" into the little vial of preservative, all I could do was laugh. Were they kidding? Was someone watching through a hidden camera for entertainment? There had to be a better way! After that silliness was over and I turned in the samples, I left the health center and headed home, confident that I would soon have a healthy, smoothly functioning digestive tract. I would have the results of the tests in two weeks.

I saw C a couple more times before I left Veiltown. The first time was at a Starbucks near the campus, maybe three weeks after our date. I was sitting and talking with a friend of mine named Jeanette. We had dated during third year. She had taken some initiative when an opportunity arose for her to meet me, and I appreciated it. I respected her, and I made it a point to remain friends with her after I broke off our romantic endeavors. I'm still happy that I did, as we have grown close. That never could have happened had I not chosen to continue knowing her, despite the fact that I didn't want to date her. It had been a while since we had met up, and I was telling her about the awful date I had been through three weeks earlier. Right on cue, in walked the heartbreaker herself. It didn't bother me, although I did take the opportunity to point her out to Jeanette. C soon left with her drink as Jeanette and I continued our conversation.

The next time I saw her was just after my memorable trip to the health center. I had left the gym after a workout and was headed to the parking lot to hop in my car. I walked right past her. She was out of shape again; her stomach was big and round, and her shoulders were slouching. But besides those changes, there was something else that was much more out of place. As she walked, she talked on her phone. I could see that the conversation wasn't a happy one. Her eyes looked melancholy, and her demeanor was that of someone who was dealing with a painful issue. I figured it must have had something to do with a "boy." Maybe I was wrong about the reasons why, but she was different than the woman I had been so infatuated with. It made me feel bad... What could I do though? I had burned any bridges to her. Besides, I wasn't ready to admit that I was in the wrong at all for lashing out. She deserved it. Everything I said was true, and sometimes the truth can be cruel. It didn't matter anyhow. Her feelings were out of my hands.

About two weeks after my trip to the health center, I arrived home in the evening to find that I had a voicemail message. I hadn't had time to even look at my phone throughout the day because I had been so busy. When I checked the message, the voice on the other end sounded happy to relay that all of the tests came up negative—meaning that I didn't have an infection or a parasite of any kind. I didn't know what to think. I just sat on my bed, reeling from the news. "No… What is it then?" I thought to myself. Having an education in the healthcare field can be frightening at times. You know that major, life-threatening diseases are rare, but you also know that they exist far better than the average person does. That makes it somewhat stressful when you have symptoms you can't explain, especially after diagnostic tests. My mind ran amuck, imagining what exactly my ailment could be if it couldn't be attributed to invasion by another organism. I had to get to a hot Yoga class that I had been attending in the next few minutes though, so I got changed, picked up my gear, and took off.

On the short drive to the studio, I worried. Exactly how sick was I? Did I have some digestive disease, like Crohn's, or Irritable Bowel Syndrome, or was it something far worse? Did I have cancer? None of it sounded appealing, but I was particularly worried about cancer. I hadn't been the healthiest eater throughout my life. I just had a high metabolism and worked out a lot, so I looked and felt healthy. Maybe all those cheeseburgers had finally taken their toll. Maybe I had damaged myself—who knew how badly?

When I got to the studio, my thinking had deteriorated to the point where I was consumed with the idea that I might have cancer. Cancer wouldn't beat me though. Screw that. If I had it, I would beat IT. I would be one of those people who cancer couldn't kill, try as it might. No way was I going to give up my life because of fast food. I asked the instructor if she believed in the powers of Yoga to heal cancer. She said that she did and then asked me why I wanted to know. I told her that I was concerned that I might have cancer. If that was so, I was going to find a way out, and I had heard that Yoga and the spiritual peace it could provide were believed to be potent healers. I had even heard that Yoga had helped people overcome extremely severe cancers in the past. She was concerned. She asked me why I thought I might have the disease. I told her about the problems I had been having for the last four months and how they had been getting worse. I also told her about how the diagnostic tests had come up negative. After my explanation, she suggested a laughable concept to me. She asked me if I had been under any stress as of late. In my mind, I scoffed at that: "Me? Stress?" She obviously didn't know how strong I was. I always appreciated life, and I was always happy. Yeah, I had just gone through a few months of ups and downs and ultimately a major disappointment, but that was life. I could deal. I WAS dealing. "Stress... Yeah right," I thought. I told her I didn't think that was it. She went on to tell me a story about how she had gone through some major digestive issues about a year before, eventually undertaking a huge battery of tests that found nothing. She would have sworn that she wasn't overly stressed out, but in the end, she discovered that she was. As soon as she started to calm down and put things into perspective, she started feeling better. I thought about it for a second, but dismissed the idea. I knew myself well, and stress wasn't the cause of this. I was sure of it. We had to cut our conversation short because class was about to begin.

The next day, I had the afternoon off and I called to schedule an appointment with a gastroenterologist (a doctor who specializes in the digestive system). I was absolutely shocked to find that I would have to wait two whole months for the appointment. Great! With cancer, early detection is key. You never know how much time you have before you pass a point of unlikely recovery. I had heard some frightening stories about healthcare in Canada. According to some, the docket there is so packed that people die while waiting to be seen. Was that going to happen to me? I couldn't fight if I didn't have the treatment I needed to help me along. I was getting pretty worried.

When DJ got home at dusk, I was sitting in the shadows on the couch with a blank look on my face. He immediately asked what was wrong. I hadn't told him about the test results the night before because I didn't want to worry him unnecessarily. Now I was terrified. I needed to tell him, so I did. Then I told him about how my Yoga teacher had suggested that it might be stress. I knew that was preposterous. DJ sort of raised an eyebrow at that. "What?" I asked. "You know me man. I don't stress." He replied, "Maybe not normally, but you haven't been quite yourself since... well, you know." I was instantly indignant, but too drained to blow up. "C'mon man. I'm over that shit." "Are you?" he returned. "Of course I am," I replied. "Okay... So what if it's cancer?" he asked. "What do you think? I fight." DJ nodded his head. He reached out his hand and we gave each other daps. DJ... I'm pretty sure he knew. If he did, he also knew that I would only figure it out on my own, so he didn't push it.

33

The Truth

Maybe a week or so later, I woke up early in the morning in a lot of pain. My stomach was killing me. Besides that, the only thing on my mind was C. I had been mulling over my life since the day my lab results came back, and C had been on my mind quite a bit more lately. I wasn't angry with her; I never really had been. It was just a knee-jerk reaction to not being able to be with her. I didn't get what I wanted, so I threw a fit, in a manner of speaking. I felt the most overpowering sense of remorse for what I had done. As I lay there, I finally started to put it all together. Truthfully, I had thought about C every day since the date, if only for seconds at a time, and my digestion had been getting worse and worse; so had the pain. Then I got it—the problem had started soon after I had called C for the first time and she subsequently began ignoring me. After a little contemplation over the matter, I remembered that my symptoms would get worse when things were going bad with her and better when things were good. Since our date, my symptoms had only gotten worse; and when I would think about her, the physical pain would be excruciating. "My God," I thought. It was stress:

stress over C. The fact that I had been so cruel to her just added on a terrible, festering guilt. All I wanted was to make it right.

I wrote C another e-mail. I didn't want to leave a voicemail, and there was no way on earth she would answer. I knew that. The e-mail was short. I told her how guilty I felt, and that there is never a good reason to be mean to someone. I also let her know that I had realized that she was trying to be nice by going out with me; I couldn't blame her for the fact that her heart wasn't in it. I apologized, and I offered her my friendship, if she would take it. As I sent the letter off, I felt a great pressure lift from me. I would say that it was a relief, but underneath the pressure, I had buried the truth: I was devastated.

Healing… a long, difficult road. I had to right the wrong that I had done to C, and I had to face the pain I was in so I could deal with it. Little by little, I would cry it out: in bed at night, in the shower in the morning, walking in the halls at school trying hard to keep anyone from noticing. It helped, but my heart still railed against the thought of never getting to hold C in my arms. Her name resounded in my head. I prayed against all logic that she would write me back and accept my offer of friendship. I would be a great friend to her; she would see. I could get to her that way. I wouldn't even have to be assertive. In the end, I knew that she would be the one who would instigate our life together because even though she didn't know it, I was the one for her. To my great disappointment, the days passed and I was unwillingly forced to accept what I really already knew: I was hoping against hope. This time, there would be no reply. C just didn't care about me.

Although I was incapable of letting go, I actually did feel better a few weeks later. Funny how storing up emotion can almost rip you apart, but if you let it out, things most often get better. Encouragingly, my digestion was improving day-by-day. I felt better about other aspects of my life as well. To my surprise, as school was coming to an end, I had the twisted thought that I might even miss some parts of it. I had really begun to enjoy the patient care aspect of dentistry, and my focus was always sharp when I had another human being in my chair. After all, I owed them my best. Besides that, although I sometimes felt that the entire city (save for DJ and Darren) was against me, I realized that I did like some of my classmates quite a bit. In fact, I liked most everybody (even if many of them couldn't say the same about me). I even liked Alan. We had started out on the wrong foot, but after four years, I could see that he was actually a real good guy. Slowly, we had been able to reconcile our differences, and I was appreciative that we were able to get past our initial unpleasantness towards each other. After all, I didn't need any more enemies.

34

Closure

I wanted to make some sort of a mark as I left school, so I suggested to Darren that we should compose and perform a hip-hop number about dental school for the annual talent show. The show was to be held about a month before graduation, and Darren agreed to rap with me. We spent two straight weeks of nights writing lyrics, getting the music ready, and rehearsing. It was crazy fun just preparing, and the show was even better; we brought the house down. The crowd of dental students, faculty, and staff who came to watch went nuts. Performing was such a rush, and that was what my life really needed: some good emotion (even if it was only temporary). Darren and I grew that much closer because of it too. What could be better? We both got all sorts of compliments about the show over the next week.

Mason (of all people) told Darren that he was impressed by our performances. I had laced into Mason just a few months earlier because he wrote an e-mail to the entire class, cryptically bragging about his acceptance into an oral surgery program. I felt he had been incredibly insensitive to the people in our class who had been denied acceptance into specialty programs, and I wrote him an e-mail telling him that someone needed to smack him. Then, I brought his actions to the attention of the faculty. They had some choice words for him as well. After I had gotten him in trouble, I was perplexed at his compliment, to say the least. Maybe he was trying to reach out to me. I didn't really care if he was. He was still worthless as far as I was concerned.

As graduation neared, I felt myself looking for reasons to stay in Veiltown. I hoped that maybe I would find a great girl who would make me think twice about moving. I honestly was trying to move on. Things ended with Karen a couple of weeks after school let out. It was fun while it lasted, but we had some differences that couldn't be reconciled, and I wouldn't have stayed for her anyhow. I stepped up my search and hit on quite a few women that I thought were up to snuff. No luck though—just more bad dates and phone messages never to be replied to.

After almost nine months of simmering over it, I was ready to apologize to Errol. I missed him. When I thought back to second year and how his friendship had been such a help to me, I decided that being his friend was more important than being prideful or winning some silly argument over a broken door. I called him one day and apologized. He was a big person and apologized for his part in the disagreement as well. I appreciated that more than he could know. I didn't want to be right. I just wanted him to meet me halfway. He came through for me, just as he had during second year.

DJ took off for Japan right after the quarter was over. He had a nice internship lined up, and he would get to spend some time with his girlfriend, Ayako. They had met in Japan when he was studying abroad at the end of college. Later, when DJ went back to teach English, they had developed a romance and fallen in love. Just as two loyal people would, they stayed together when he came back to the states. He hadn't proposed yet, but they planned to be married in the future. Although I was happy that DJ had a chance to spend some time with Ayako, I was also sad to see him go. We had lived together for two years, and he was the best roommate I ever had. I wasn't surprised. I knew I would miss living with him, talking about things, and just plain kickin' it. On the day he left, we hugged each other tight, the same way we had when he left home for college in Southern California so many years ago. I watched him drive down the street as a tear rolled off my cheek. I would have never gotten through those times without his help. Because of that, he has my loyalty more than ever.

On graduation day, I woke up and just didn't want to go. I felt depressed, and I finally had the wherewithal to admit it to myself. I had planned to attend the ceremony, but instead I drove to the student union building on the main campus and returned my rented gown. Then I went to Macy's and shopped a little. It was therapeutic. While I was shopping, I got two phone calls. First, my buddy George called to see if I was okay. George had been in the class ahead of mine, and we had become pretty good friends during the last couple of years. When he graduated, he had gone into the pediatric dentistry program at our school. He was assigned to a site in a small farming community about two hours east of Veiltown, and I had spent some time with him while on a two-week pediatric dentistry rotation there during the time when I was waiting for C's season to be over. George had recently married a classmate of mine named Leela. She had also become a pretty good friend. When George called, he informed me that Leela was really concerned to see that I wasn't at graduation and that she worried that I had gotten into an accident. I assured him that I was alright and that I just felt too depressed to show up. He begrudgingly accepted my reasons and let me go. Next Kyle, another of my classmates, called and told me that everybody was wondering where I was. I told him I was at Macy's. He urged me to hurry down for the ceremony, but I told him I had already returned my gown. I was glad to hear from him and thanked him for his concern. We hung up, and I got back to browsing through dress-shirts and slacks. I felt a little better after that. Maybe a few people liked me after all.

My time in Veiltown went rapidly after that. I wasn't concerned with the clinical board examination in the least. Even with all of the garbage we had faced at dental school, we were well prepared to pass the test. I kept a relaxed attitude as I took the exam and passed it easily. It seemed that most of my class was extremely worried and nervous before the test, but most of them passed in spite of their fear. As far as I know, two people failed and had to retake the exam at a later date. No big deal. I'm sure they passed the second time around. With boards complete, I was happy to have one more trifle out of the way.

Our landlord had been kind enough to let DJ and I out of our lease early so he could go to Japan without having to pay another two months of rent. It was for the better anyhow because I couldn't have paid my share due to the dwindling balance in my checking account. I didn't want to go to Idaho to stay with my parents after boards were over, but I couldn't afford to pay anyone for a room. Darren and his roommates were kind enough to let me crash on a couch they had in the loft area upstairs. I stayed for about a month. In late July, I had run out of funds and had no way to earn any more. I had no choice but to head for my parents' place in Nampa, Idaho.

The day before I left, I tried to get a last workout in at the university's gym. Unfortunately, they had special hours that day; I was unaware and missed my opportunity. After being stoned at the gym entrance, I walked back to my car, which I had parked in the local shopping center's parking lot earlier. On my way, I ran into Paige. She had just come from Starbucks. She relayed a peculiar story about the clerk there accusing her of having pinkeye and asked me if I thought her eye looked red. I didn't see anything at all. Her story and the way she was flustered about it were pretty comical, and I was entertained. What was more, she was very friendly and open with me—much more so than the first time we had spoken after our date. She even asked me advice about some dental care she had recently received. It felt nice to interact with her in such a pleasant way. I asked if she still planned to move to Los Angeles. She said she wanted to, but she needed to figure out just how she would swing it. I had been thinking about something since I had discovered Paige might come to LA, and I decided to run it by her. I told her about how I had been taking private dance lessons since early in the year. I was going to keep taking lessons when I got to LA, so I offered to let her come and be my partner, as private lessons cost the same for one person as they do for a couple. I remembered how Paige liked to dance, and I wanted to reach out to her and try to further repair the friendship that I felt we could have built. She was pleased at the offer, so I told her I would e-mail her and let her know how everything was progressing as I made my way to Southern California. I could tell by her body language that she was cool with that. We parted, and I made it to my car and drove back to Darren's place.

Saying goodbye to Darren was just as hard as saying goodbye to DJ. His friendship too had protected me through many cold, rainy nights. One night, not long before I left, we were in his car headed home after hanging out downtown and he told me that when we had first talked on the phone, he was somewhat taken aback by my blunt assertion that we could be good friends. He went on to tell me that after two years of living in Veiltown, he truly understood why I came on so strongly: he felt my pain. Misery loves company, and through that misery we built a bond that I know will never be broken. As I drove out of the city, I reflected that I had found my reasons for coming to Veiltown: one old friend, one new. Much love fellas…

35

The Eye of the Storm

Before I had left Veiltown, I entertained the idea of giving one last-ditch effort at winning C over. She didn't know who I was, and that was the problem. I was certain that if I could make her understand me somehow, she would change her mind. I knew that the chances of that were slim to non-existent, but well, you'll never know unless you try, right? I wrote a couple of e-mail letters that I thought might be convincing enough, but I never sent either. I showed one of them to my friend Lana. We had met through a mutual acquaintance a couple of years before, and she had become a trusted confidant. We shared a lot of frustration about love, and she was usually behind me on my decisions. This time was different. She asked me, "What do you think sending her this will accomplish?" All I could answer was, "Nothing..." She was right—C wouldn't care. I left Veiltown carrying the feeling that I had made a dire mistake, but I had no idea how to correct it

I spent the next month with my parents in Idaho. It was good to see them again, but Idaho was as it always has been for me: boring. I don't have anything against it, by any means, but I'm a city boy, and Idaho is all country. I'm just not into the lifestyle there. On top of my normal qualms about being there, it was even worse this particular time because I didn't socialize at all. There was no point in meeting anyone. I was going to leave as soon as I could get my California dental license. (That would be around September.) It wouldn't really make sense to socialize. Boredom aside, it was the first time I had been back to that place since Jake died. As time had passed, I had healed to some extent, but I still felt guilty. When I arrived, it all came rushing back to me: how careless I had been and how I let my puppy die because I was too tired to go outside with him. The first time I visited Jake's grave, I collapsed in the dirt and sobbed. I could move on, but I knew I would never truly forgive myself.

I got a membership at a Gold's gym that was about thirty minutes away from my parents' house, and I spent my days exercising and writing. I went to the gym five or six days every week and each day I worked on a writing project I got the idea for while I was still in Veiltown. I clipped along and got quite a bit written. Thankfully, my being so busy with exercise and my writings helped the time pass pretty rapidly.

I had to go back to Veiltown for my appointment with the gastroenterologist just two weeks after I had left. It was a short trip. When I talked with the doctor, I told him about what had happened and how my symptoms had been steadily improving. I wasn't completely back to normal, but I was much better. He wasn't concerned after hearing what I had to say, and he told me to keep monitoring it; if things worsened, I should get it checked out again. I was glad to see that I was doing a better job of dealing with my sorrow.

I thought about C when my mind wasn't focused on those other things, and the feeling that I had made a huge mistake only grew. I couldn't shake the emotions that I felt for her, no matter how I tried to reason with myself or rationalize them away. I wanted to be over her... I tried to convince myself that I just needed time, and that once things started rolling with my new life, I wouldn't have much time to dwell on the past. After a while though, I knew that it wasn't going to happen. It was like trying to convince myself that my favorite color was inappropriate, or that I shouldn't like watching football. I can't really tell you why I like the color red, or football, but I can tell you that they make me happy. That was exactly the way I felt about C. How do you change feelings? I know a lot of people won't understand why I would feel this way about a woman I didn't know. Some might even think that my state would be something that should be thought of as "sad." (I probably would have agreed before I met C.) The only thing I can really say about it now is that you won't truly understand until you feel something like it yourself; there is no way to explain it. Even after C had hurt me, I could only truly feel good emotions about her. She hadn't done anything mean to me. She had been inconsiderate of my feelings, perhaps, but everyone is guilty of that in relation to other people at some point in their lives. To be fair, I was starting to really understand how I had turned her off to me, so I couldn't blame her, even for lying. As I have said before, people's actions are often situational, and I know from experience that you can't make sweeping generalizations about people based on their behavior in just one situation. In short, there was no foothold for me to climb away from C. Anger and spite would have given me one, but I didn't feel either. I had no choice but to live with it.

Something that eased the pain a bit was my newfound friendship with Paige. I e-mailed her a few days after I got to Nampa, and we had been corresponding ever since. She was such an expressive writer, and reading her letters was like reading a great piece of literature. I would always perk up just a bit when I would open my e-mail account to find a message from her in the inbox. When I wrote to her, I would generally make my letters as long (and as funny) as I could. One time I sent her a silly little response to an e-mail she had written about meeting a guy who she thought was my twin. I told her that I was born a Siamese twin and had been attached to my brother at the butt-cheek. Then I expanded on it. I felt a sense of triumph when she wrote back to me, and the first line of the letter was, "You are so funny!" It made me feel so much better inside because I was proving to myself what I had felt all along: I was worth taking the time to know.

DJ had been planning to go to visit his mother and brother for a few weeks when he got back from Japan. I had known about his plans before he left, but I didn't have any plans to go with him, especially because I was flat broke and my parents were supporting me while I waited for my dental license. To my delight, one day I looked at one of my credit card balances to find that I had been given two thousand more dollars worth of credit. I was getting really tired of Idaho, and now I could afford to go home with DJ. I hadn't been there in a while, and it would be good to see his family and our friends who still lived there. I asked him if it would be cool if I came, and he said yes. Great! Soon I could get out of that place.

A couple weeks before I headed back to Veiltown to meet DJ, my mother and I were talking. As we had done so many times before, we started to argue. My father was out of town on business for the week. He didn't like arguments to go on when he was around, but without him there, I had the freedom to argue as much as I wanted. My mother didn't like to be criticized, but I had some things to say to her, and they were going to be said, whether she liked it or not. After we had been yelling at each other for a few minutes, she did what she always did when we argued: she tried to leave. I wouldn't let her. She picked up her keys and her purse and headed for the door. I stood in front of it. She tried to exit through another door, but I stopped her from opening it. Eventually, after trying fruitlessly to escape a few more times, she went into her bathroom and closed the door. I stood by the door and waited for her to come out. I told her I would wait all day because we had some things to discuss; I wasn't going to leave her alone until they were resolved. These were issues that had lingered between us for many years. After a while, she got very angry and opened the door to the bathroom, yelling and demanding that I let her leave. I just stood in her way. Then she pushed me, but I didn't budge. Next, she slapped me in the face. I just looked at her. She slapped me again, which made me a bit perturbed, so I took my fingertips and sort of pushed her cheek in return for the slaps. That infuriated her, but she couldn't do anything about it other than scream at me. I stood there in the doorway, not letting her pass. I knew that if I could hold out long enough, she would get exhausted and stop screaming. (It takes a lot of energy to make loud noises with one's mouth!) Eventually, she didn't have the will to scream anymore. We started to talk, and maybe for the first time in our lives, we had a productive conversation about us. I explained to her how she had scarred me by favoring my sister when we were growing up and how I didn't feel like she ever really appreciated anything I had done. Why was it that having kids was such a great accomplishment, but graduating from dental school wasn't nearly as important? Any physiologically advanced twelve-year-old could bear a child. Not that I was trying to knock my sister's life, but I felt sad that my mother didn't really seem to care about the things I did. To her credit, she actually listened to me, rather than denying it. To be fair, I acknowledged all the ways she had shown her love for me too. I wasn't blind. I made sure that she understood how much I loved her and appreciated what she had given me. In return, she told me how she really was proud of the things I did and how proud she was to tell other people when they asked what I was doing. We talked calmly for a long time. I think we finally started to understand each other… after more than twenty-eight years.

DJ got back to Veiltown a short while after that, and I headed up to meet him. My parents wanted me to stay with them, but there was no way that was going to happen. I was going to die if I didn't get some social interaction, and what better way than with DJ, Ansel, and Mike? Even Dustin was going to be in town for a few days. I wish… I had stayed with my parents. Regrettably, I can't change it now. A couple days after I got to Veiltown, DJ and I hopped in his car and made our way home.

It had been about two years since I had been back, and it was good to see Mike, Ansel, and Dustin again. The five of us had some great times just hanging out and talking about everything that had gone on in our lives. Ansel would soon be married to Wendy. The wedding was to be in October, and he wanted me to be his "second best man." He told me he had a rough time deciding between Dustin and me, so he made Dustin the official best man, and I would be the backup (of sorts). I was honored. The offer made me especially happy, considering our difficulties the last time we had seen each other.

The trip ended up lasting about five days longer than planned because DJ's transmission died two days before we were to return. My dental license still hadn't come through, so it wasn't a big deal; but any day now, I would become official. Once that happened, I could head for Los Angeles. The day before we left for Veiltown, I was notified that my license had been processed and I could officially start work. I just had to find a job.

As soon as we got back to Veiltown, I got in my car and headed for Nampa. I arrived at my parents' house, slept, then woke up and organized my stuff. Then I slept again, and when I woke up, I left. My mom got up to see me off. I told her I loved her and thanked her for everything before driving away into the early morning. I was glad that we had finally hashed out our differences. I was also glad to get the hell out of Idaho and start moving forward again.

When I reached the Los Angeles area, I stayed with a friend of mine named Rachelle. She and I had met when we were seven years old. She had just graduated from a dental school in the area, and we had run into each other at a licensing test over law and ethics a couple of months earlier in Sacramento. When I told her I was moving to LA, she offered to let me stay with her for a while. It was a really nice gesture, and I accepted. I stayed with her and her roommate Dana for a couple of weeks. Dana was a great lady too, and we were fast friends.

Finding a job didn't prove to be that hard. I got a full-time position as an associate dentist in south Orange County a couple of weeks after arriving. The owners seemed like nice enough people, and the staff members were also good folks. I started work shortly after getting back from a quick trip back home for Ansel's wedding.

Adjusting to a full-time work schedule was a little tough for me. Nevertheless, I was determined to get out of debt and set myself into a good position so that I could follow things that were more important to me. My job

192

would pay quite a bit of money, and it seemed that I was going to be able to take care of my debts the way I had envisioned. It was a good thing too, because I was starting to feel uneasy about the money I owed. (I really wanted to be rid of that mental burden.) I would throw as much money at my debts as I could, as quickly as I could, and I would soon only have student loans left to pay off.

I found an apartment in Laguna Beach (yes, the Laguna Beach famous for rich, maladapted teenagers making a spectacle of themselves on MTV), and I moved in. My new dwellings were right across the street from the beach and, therefore, a bit pricey. My rent ended up being twenty three hundred dollars per month. Even so, I was going to be making six figures per year at my job, so twenty eight thousand for rent didn't seem like that big of a deal, especially considering the location. I mean, I could see the ocean from the front window. It was cool!

If only life were predictable… At first, everything unfolded encouragingly. Although I was somewhat fatigued from all of the long workdays, I was eating well and exercising regularly. I would run through the water along the main beach in Laguna three times per week. Paige and I continued to correspond over e-mail, and we had even started to call each other once in a while. I had also made some new friends. I met a really cool cat at the Gold's Gym in Hollywood when I was staying with Rachelle. His name was John, and he was a screenwriter. We got along really well, and we started getting together every few weeks for sushi up in Hollywood. I also had Rachelle and Dana, and they introduced me to Dana's brother Ron. I started hanging out with Ron up in LA County just about every week. It was a pretty long drive, but I liked visiting LA, and Ron was a good dude. I guess friends are where you find them.

When I started spending time with Ron, my digestion started to worsen again. I wondered if I was a little stressed out, but after some contemplation, I decided that it really couldn't be the case. I felt good. Yes, I was a bit fatigued, but my attitude was positive, and I was looking forward to getting everything where it needed to be. Predictably, I was still thinking about C, but it wasn't so troublesome. I didn't get why I was having problems again. My digestion had never been back to normal, but it had gotten significantly better over the time I was in Idaho. It was vexing that my condition was deteriorating again. For sure, it was an unneeded stressor in my life, and as time went by, the symptoms continued to worsen.

When I moved to Southern California, I felt strongly compelled to right an old wrong. When I was around nineteen and Mara had just started college, she made a friend at her workplace on campus. Gina and I disliked each other immediately. In truth, my dislike of her was in response to her unprovoked dislike of me. I felt a nasty vibe from her the very first time we met, and I continued to feel it as time passed. Despite our disdain for one another, we interacted cordially for four years. I had certain ideas about Gina, and Gina had certain ideas about me. Those ideas kept us disliking each other, yet somehow, we got along. In my last semester of college, Gina's boyfriend Daniel and I moved into an apartment together. Daniel was an easygoing type: always cracking jokes and messing around. We got along well. After a few months, Gina had a falling out with her father and subsequently moved in with us. Interestingly enough, after a few weeks of living together, her vibe toward me changed. I didn't feel like she disliked me anymore. I didn't dislike her either. She was actually pretty nice, to my surprise. Maybe that was all we needed—just some time together to figure each other out. There was, however, a complication: I didn't like the way she interacted with Daniel. She was bossy and impatient with him, and I could see that he was rapidly becoming more and more unhappy. One day, I could tell Daniel was down and I suggested to him that he should break up with Gina. It was only my opinion, but I thought that she was making him unhappy and that he would be better off leaving her and moving back to the east coast (where he had been attending college before they met). After thinking it over, he agreed. Later in the evening, he did it—he broke up with her.

Gina was NOT happy. Daniel didn't tell her anything about our conversation, but she was suspicious of me anyhow. She came to me with daggers in her eyes and asked me what I had said to him. She did it with such conviction that I was sure Daniel had told her about the advice I had given him. It didn't really matter if he did. I was willing to stand by what I said, so I incriminated myself by admitting that I had advised Daniel to end things with her. We stood in the kitchen and argued for a few minutes. Gina took the stance that it was none of my business and that I should just stay out of things that didn't concern me. I took the stance that Daniel was my friend. I cared about him and his happiness, and she was making him unhappy. It didn't escalate into yelling, but I knew that we were no longer going to get along.

The two of them ended up staying together, and Gina did something unselfish by moving to the east coast with Daniel soon after. Mara and I visited with them back home around a year and a half later. Gina and I were cordial, once again, but I could see the disdain she held for me very plainly. I held the same in return. Mara and Gina continued to keep in touch, and through Mara, I learned that Gina had eventually moved to Los Angeles and then broken up with Daniel. Funny how things turned around… At any rate, I knew Gina was living there when I moved to the area.

It was mostly due to my inner turmoil and the blame I placed on myself for not being able to make many good friends in Veiltown that I contacted Gina. I wanted to do something good. I wanted to turn it around with her. I wanted to care about her and forgive her for the things I thought she did wrong in the past. I hoped she could do the same for me. I knew she would be resistant to the idea, but I felt that I could make her into a friend. I was certain that we could get along if we could only understand each other better.

I got Gina's number from Mara and called her a couple of times. I left some messages, but I figured that she wouldn't call me back. I knew I was going to have to get her to answer the phone at some point. One day, I got a call from Daniel. He said that Gina had called and told him that I had left her a message and that she assumed I was actually trying to get a hold of him. I was happy to hear from him as we had lost touch, but I told him that I did in fact want to talk to

Gina. We talked a bit, and when we got off the phone, he promised he would relay what I told him to Gina. I waited about a week to see if she would call, but she didn't, so I called her again one evening.

When she answered, she was surprised to find me on the other end of the line. The first thing I told her was not to hang up. She obliged, and then we argued for probably thirty minutes. Gina saw no reason for us to be friends. I disagreed. I was patient and let her say everything she had to say, but I was also persistent. I kept working at it until she agreed to let me come up and meet with her for coffee. That night, we sat in her apartment and chatted until around one AM. With that, we started an unlikely friendship.

Gina and I spent a good amount of time together after that. Usually, we talked about deeper things: life, love, career, self-improvement, and the like. We grew close relatively quickly, and I was pleasantly surprised at how well it was all working out. We even spent Thanksgiving Day together. She was so much more worth knowing than I had once thought. I would giggle to myself sometimes when I would leave Gina and we would hug. "Imagine this," I thought.

Things were looking up. I was making good money, I liked my job (as well as I could like a full-time regular job), I was in good health, and I had friends to talk to and spend time with. They were good friends too. Nonetheless, I still didn't have someone special in my life, and in my heart, I couldn't deny that only one woman would do. Not being one to fail from inaction, in late November, I decided to take another shot at winning C over. I had been reflecting back on my time in Veiltown a lot, and I was starting to understand the extent to which my personality had been altered there. I had really not been myself, and that was even more apparent in my interactions with C. I just wanted so badly to impress her, but I couldn't because I was afraid to offend her by being too much myself. Other people in Veiltown didn't like me, so why would she unless I acted properly? Now I was getting back to being me again: confident and motivated to find happiness. If I could just show her... I knew what I was up against, but I had to try. If I didn't, I would always regret it. Little did I know, starting with that decision, I was about to go through the most trying time in my life and I was going to catch it from every possible angle. Had I known, I would have been able to brace myself. I really thought that things were going to be much better and easier once I got to Southern California, and that it would be a rather permanent change. After all that suffering in Veiltown, things had to get better, right? Nope. I believe the next eight months taught me more about myself than any previous period in my life, and the lessons would come via no other means than baptism by fire.

36

Before It Gets Better...

I have always had very powerful emotions. When I played league basketball before high school, I used to get lots of technical fouls for arguing with the referees, spiking the ball into the court, etc. One time I got one for slamming the ball off another kid's head so it would go out of bounds. In retrospect, I won't deny that I didn't mind the fact that he fell to the ground and began to cry. That was me: emotional, reactive, impulsive, fiery, rash. Encouragingly, as I have gotten older, I have learned to control the raging tempest of emotions I feel on a daily basis. Occasionally, I'll lose control, but I get better and better at sorting things out without making self-destructive mistakes. Constitutionally, however, I am still the same inside. I still feel things much more intensely than most others do. This could be considered a weakness, and would by many, but I choose to see it as a strength. My emotions drive me to do what's right and to be a better person, and when I love, I love all the way. I wouldn't hesitate to take a bullet for the people who are important to me. I hope they know that I'll be there in a heartbeat when they need me. I don't believe that anything that can drive a person to such actions can be a bad thing.

I guess I should have thought just a little harder before I made my next move. Unfortunately for me, as I have just explained, my emotions still get the best of me from time to time. When I think about what I did now, my stomach churns. I'm almost too embarrassed to write about it. I just hope that as you read this, you'll try to understand the emotions that drove me to such a foolish action.

Following C's progress over the Internet had gotten me familiar with the names and faces of some of her teammates. One in particular was apparently an extraordinary girl. Sally was an amazing gymnast—by far the best on the team. She routinely won events that she competed in. Everything I had ever read about her had been positive and glowing. Sally had actually graduated the year before. While I was in Veiltown, I had seen her at the gym talking with C a few times. I liked her demeanor a lot. She just seemed like a pretty stand-up gal, so being at a loss for ideas on what to do, I decided to attempt to recruit her to help me with C. No, I had never met her. Yes, I am aware of how ridiculous this idea sounds, but all I could think about at the time was figuring out a way to get to C. I looked up Sally's e-mail address, and I sent her a letter.

I was a bit cryptic in that letter as I tried to gauge how Sally would respond to my overtures, seeing as how they came out of the blue. Basically, I told her that I needed her help on something, but I didn't say what. I also didn't really explain who I was. I told her I had chosen to ask for her assistance because I knew of her and thought she seemed like a really nice person. I wanted for her to e-mail with me a bit, and I would explain what I wanted from her. I can see how this could be, and WAS a bit frightening to a young woman. She probably thought I was trying to lure her into some situation where I could attack her. I guess I would have thought the same if I were her and I got an e-mail like that. Notwithstanding how obvious that should have been, my actions were guided by the fact that I knew I wasn't dangerous or crazy; I was only compelled by the most powerful feelings for C. In my mind, the truth was the only thing that was important, and I was certain that it would shine through in the end. Perception…

A few days passed, and there was no reply. (Do you see a pattern here?) I talked with DJ about it, and he suggested that I just write another e-mail and lay it all out for her. It was a good suggestion, given the circumstances, so I took his advice. I wrote her another letter. This time, I apologized and then told her who I was and why I needed her help. I explained some things that I thought she should know: like how I had to stop my hands from trembling before I first spoke with C and how I had these irrational and unfounded but completely magical feelings for her. I told Sally how I had gone through some problems in Veiltown, and how I had not been able to be myself with C because of the damage those problems had caused. I needed Sally's help because I had no avenue to communicate with C. I had no way to show her who I really was. She was distant and unwilling to listen to me. I just didn't have any options. I told her that I had a plan, and the only way it could work was with her help. I figured she would reply, now that I was being clearer. I also knew that her response would probably be negative. Nonetheless, I hung onto the hope that I could change my fate and turn everything around.

The reply came quickly. I was afraid to read it, so I had Gina do it for me. Gina came to me with a pained look in her eyes after she read the message. I knew what it meant. "Bad?" I asked. "Bad…" she responded. At least the anticipation was over. I wanted to know the heartbreaking specifics, so I read it. The message was short and to the point. Sally told me she had spoken with C and that she was "not interested in a relationship with me." Then she told me how she was sorry, but "sometimes things don't go the way we want them to." I had to smile at receiving life-lessons from a woman who was six years younger than me. Afterwards, she told me not to contact anymore of C's friends. That really didn't need to be said, but I could understand where she was coming from. At any rate, she was polite in the letter, and I appreciated it. I sent her back a "thank you." Once again, I sat in defeat, on the verge of tears.

Gina was a real friend that night. We were at her apartment, and she let me hang around and spill my feelings to her for a long time. She even gave me some of the oatmeal cookies that she was baking for a social group she was part of. Gina knew the whole story by that point, and she asked if I was going to be able to let go after this latest setback. I didn't know. She had been against me contacting C again at all. She said it would make me seem obsessed and dangerous. For those who don't know, the definition of *obsess*, according to Merriam-Webster's Collegiate Dictionary is: "to haunt or excessively preoccupy the mind of" ("Obsess" def.) Many people are obsessed with something in their lives. A professional athlete is obsessed with his or her sport, a doctor is obsessed with his job, and many children are obsessed with video games. Being obsessed isn't necessarily a bad thing. It can be productive. Thomas Edison was obsessed with creating the light bulb, and Martin Luther King Jr. was obsessed with civil rights. Get the point? I have no issue with admitting that I was obsessed, but I was absolutely not dangerous: never that. Regardless, the night's events had left me deflated. As difficult as it was for me to even entertain the idea of letting go, I was starting to believe that maybe I should. I really didn't want to frighten C, and I could see by Sally's response that things were heading in that direction. Gina and I talked late into the night, and she let me crash on her couch. It was a great comfort to be there with her.

37

Downward Spiral

I took Sally's response hard—harder than I thought I would. It gnawed at my heart. I started having a lot more trouble sleeping than usual. "How could all this have happened?" I thought. I had been so sure. Every bit of who I was told me that I needed to be with C. But now, how could I keep trying? How could I keep believing after what had happened?

The next few weeks passed rather painfully, but I had Gina and John, as well as DJ, Mike, Mara, Ansel, and Darren to talk to about my problems. (I hadn't told Ron about this aspect of my life yet.) They were all just as supportive as they could be, but realistic at the same time. They were concerned about my emotional state, and the consensus seemed to be that I might be better off if I could throw in the towel and walk away. I was just so tired of suffering. Maybe giving up was the smartest thing to do.

At that same point in time, my mother was getting ready to go into surgery. She had a large benign tumor in her uterus that had been there for a few years, and it would require a hysterectomy to remove it. Mom was apprehensive about the surgery. Her physician had monitored the tumor for years as it remained the same size, but it had recently begun growing, so he advised that she should have it removed as soon as possible. She grudgingly consented, and the surgery was to be performed on December eighteenth. She also had two hernias that needed to be repaired, and the surgeons were to handle them during the same session. Of course, I worried about her. My mother wasn't the healthiest person on earth, and I knew the procedure would be taxing on her. I was looking forward to the surgery being over with. It would be a relief when she was on the road to recovery.

The gymnastics season would be starting in a few weeks, at the beginning of January. C's team had its first meet in Los Angeles, and before I sent the letters to Sally, I had considered going to watch. I wanted to see C perform. She had denied me her permission to do so during the last season, but I was thinking that maybe I could go to the meet and stay out of her sight. Then I sent that stupid letter. I couldn't go after that. If C were to see me there, she would probably panic, and I would never forgive myself if I interfered with something that was so important to her. Besides, what good could come of it? It definitely wouldn't help me get over her, if that was what I was going to try to do.

On the eighteenth, I called my mom in the evening. She had come through the surgery successfully and was in recovery. She sounded drugged up and exhausted. When I heard her voice, I got choked up. We talked for a few minutes about how she was feeling and the standard post-surgery things. I had been on her back for probably ten years about changing her lifestyle habits and getting healthier. The thought of her mortality had struck fear deep inside of me, and I didn't want to see her suffer as she aged. She hadn't changed though. She just kept rationalizing her bad habits, and they had taken more and more of a toll as the years had passed. She had experienced a myriad of issues in recent years, and I was afraid that her death would come sooner than later. Maybe it was a combination of all of those things that had made me so uneasy about the procedure. Despite my fears, it had to be done, and I was relieved to hear my mother's voice that night.

While we were talking, a loud beeping started, and my mother told me to hold on. I was immediately terrified. I started calling into the phone: "Mom? Mom! Mom!!! What's happening?!" She got back on the line a second later and told me that the beeping came from some sort of monitor. She was supposed to breathe deeply into a tube if it went off. That calmed me a bit, but my heart was racing. We talked for a few more minutes, and I gradually calmed down. I wanted her to rest and recover, so I cut the conversation short. Before the procedure, we had been discussing her improving her lifestyle habits after the surgery was over. Once the hernias were repaired and she recovered, she could start doing some exercises to strengthen her muscles and her heart. I could tell from her tone that she wanted to do it this time. Maybe her own mortality and frailness were starting to weigh on her mind. Before I got off the phone with her, I wanted to remind her of what she had to do. I said, "See Mom? It's like you've got a new lease on life now. Right?" She replied with, "Yeah…" I told her I loved her, and we hung up.

Two days later, on a Wednesday, I awoke at four-thirty in the morning to the sound of my phone ringing. I reached for it with a terrible fear in my heart as I silently and desperately prayed. On that day, my prayers weren't to be answered. There it was: Dad. "No…" I knew exactly what it meant. I answered to find my father, ever the soldier, keeping it together. He gave me a report of sorts —quick and to the point. Mom had experienced severe difficulty breathing throughout the previous night. The doctors had tried frantically to figure out what was going wrong, as they always do, but her condition rapidly deteriorated and she had to undergo emergency surgery. They thought she had developed a blood clot in her lungs somewhere, but they couldn't locate it. The doctors gave her a fifty/fifty chance. My dad asked me if I could make it there in the next few hours. I told him I would do my best, and I let him go.

I didn't have enough money to buy a plane ticket on that particular day. I was to be paid soon, but I needed to get a flight ASAP, so I called Mara. She didn't hesitate to buy me a ticket for the next available flight to Boise. I love her so much. When a friend helps you out so willingly, you have to put it in perspective and realize that a lot of people aren't so generous. It makes you appreciate those true friends all the more. I flew out of John Wayne Airport in Orange County at around three o'clock that afternoon.

Before I made it out of Southern California, I had spoken with my sister a couple of times. At one point, she informed me that the doctors had closed Mom up and that they gave her very little chance of surviving. When I got on the plane, I knew that I was making the trip only to say goodbye...

I arrived at the airport in Boise at about ten-thirty PM. There had been a layover in San Francisco, so it took a while to get to my destination. My mother's sister Sheila picked me up at the airport, and we drove to the hospital together. My mother's kidneys had failed, and she had slipped into a coma many hours earlier. She had not shown any signs of recovering since. Sheila was heartbroken, as was I. The only things left were the formalities.

My father and sister were with my mother when we arrived at her room. I was crushed to see Mom lying in her bed with all sorts of tubes coming out of her. Her entire body was swollen, and her face looked very old to me. Her skin was bruised, and only the life-support system was preventing her passage on to the next world. When my father saw me, his eyes filled with tears, as did mine. We embraced tightly for a moment, and I spoke into his ear: "Don't you give up. Don't you dare..." Some people lose their will to go on when they lose their partner, and I didn't want my father to be one of them. There was more life to live for him; there were more experiences to be had and more good things yet to come. He just had to make it through. I turned to my mother. With tears in my eyes, I put my face near her ear and whispered, "Hi Mom... I love you. We'll see each other again. I promise." I kissed her on her forehead and stepped back to look at her, reeling from the gravity of the situation. An hour later, at midnight of

December twenty-first, we took my mother off life support. Her body took a couple of weak breaths, in a last effort to get oxygen to her heart and brain; as she exhaled, her body shuddered. With that, the last traces of her life vanished, only sixty-two years after she had first come into the world. My father, my sister, and Sheila cried as she passed on. I just stood there. I was too stunned to cry anymore. My worst fears had come true. Just as I had been warned in dental school, some people's sickly bodies couldn't withstand the stresses of surgery. My mother had died because her body was too frail, due to a lifetime of bad habits. I had tried to save her for the last ten years, but it had been for not. It was incredibly painful that I had seen this very thing coming but couldn't do anything to stop it.

Before we left the hospital, Darren called to offer me his shoulder. I had left him a message earlier in the day, but he had not been able to get back to me sooner because he was at a hospital in San Francisco with his best friend from childhood. It turns out that his friend's father had passed on to the next life just hours earlier. Darren was more than any person could ever be expected to be that day, as he did his best to watch over both of us. I pray that I will be able to be as strong for him, if and when the time comes.

My father and I drove back to the house that night and went to sleep. There was an emptiness to that place—a lack of warmth. The pictures seemed faded and the furniture cast long shadows. My father's home would never be the same again. The next morning, Dad took me to the airport. There was no leeway for me to stay and mourn with my family. I would have to do that alone. I had responsibilities.

I remember sitting in the airport, waiting to board the airplane for home. As I waited, memories ran through my mind: memories of home, and childhood, and Mom... I don't know how to explain what I was feeling. I only know that it was a feeling of cold finality and immense loss. I guess every child should live to see his or her parents pass away; it is a much crueler fate for parents to bury their children. I understood that, but it didn't take away the sadness I felt. I knew that my sister and I would have melancholy days ahead, but it was nothing compared to the pain that my father was already going through. We, as children, had no choice in who our mother would be. We were born to her, and we loved her for all the wonderful qualities she possessed, but we didn't choose her the way my father had. He had found her somehow, in this world full of people, and chosen to marry her—to have children with her and to stand by her side through many trying years. She had done the same for him. From what I know of their relationship, they had only known each other for a few months when my father proposed. They had loved each other powerfully and with conviction, and they stayed together through some terrible times that respect for my family's privacy won't allow me to describe here. They held to each other, in spite of the way the world tries to tear lovers apart. They were best friends. I sat with my head down as I quietly wept for them: for the first time they met, for their first kiss… and for the first time they made love. I waited there in the airport with great streams of tears running down my face, soaking my neck and shirt. I wonder how I looked to the people who passed by. Probably like someone who had just lost something important.

I would be remiss if I did not mention that my friend Mike and I talked for quite a while as I waited for my plane to come. He isn't a big part of this story, but he is as important a friend as I will ever have. His support meant more to me than I can ever say. That day he was incredible, as always. Mad love kid…

By the time I got home that evening, my mouth tasted like tears and I was utterly spent. What was worse, I had to go to work the next day. Through all of that, you would think that I would have gotten through at least one day without thinking of C, but that wasn't the case. There she was, front and center in my mind, somehow comforting me. I know that the last thing I was thinking about before I fell asleep that night was her.

38

If at First (and Second) You Don't Succeed…

Was it possible that things could get worse after that? Unfortunately, things can always get worse. Work turned into hell once I got back. It was the end of the year and a whole lot of patients were trying to use up their remaining dental insurance to get work done. Greedily, the practice tried to schedule as many people as possible, and that made things extremely difficult for me (especially given the state of mind I was in). I was too sad to even be at work, but I couldn't afford to not be there. What was even worse was that many of the patients I was seeing were in pain, either needing to start root canals or to have teeth extracted. Those procedures take a bit of time, and I was forced into a mad scramble to keep up. On the last Friday before the New Year, we were absolutely swamped with patients, and I was so overwhelmed that I felt like quitting on the spot. I was seeing four patients every hour, and no matter how I tried, I couldn't prevent myself from getting behind. The further behind I fell, the guiltier I felt for making people wait, and the unhappier I became. My friend Ray, the office manager, noticed what I was going through and told me to go home. He knew that I just wasn't up to what was being asked of me that day, and he understood. He told me that if his mom had just died, he wouldn't be able to deal with a day like that day either. I agreed with his appraisal. He rescheduled all of my patients, and I left. That was a huge relief. I felt bad having to inconvenience the rest of the people on my schedule, but I needed to go home.

I had not been enjoying my job at all lately, and my mother's passing had thrown me into a state of questioning. I was questioning everything, and I was having trouble reconciling some of the things I was being forced to do at that practice with the way in which I wanted to live my life. It seemed to have gotten far worse since I had come back from Idaho. That day, I began to understand what I was going to have to do. If I quit though, I would be putting myself into a bad spot financially and I knew it. I guess you can't choose the times when you will have to make tough decisions. They just come up, no matter what other things you might be struggling with at the moment.

Another tough decision that was weighing on my mind and heart was the one I had to make concerning C. I was ready to let go of it all before my mother died, but her passing made me reconsider. After all that I had been through, I could only think of one thing that could fix me. She was back in Veiltown, preparing for the start of her last season as a college athlete. My battered heart began to shut my reason down, once again. It kept telling me, "You can't give up. If you give up, you will never know if you could have won her over." I asked myself, "What if you can convince her? What if you just have to keep trying? Is there anyone out there who can give her what you can? Is she worth the risk?" I knew that there wasn't anyone else who could give her what I could; that just wasn't possible. And she was worth the risk—every bit of it. But I was afraid. The last thing I ever wanted was to frighten her or harm her in any way.

On the sixth of January, I went up Los Angeles to hang out with Gina and Daniel. They had started speaking again recently, after she had called him to give him my number. They were entertaining the idea of getting back together even. It would be a bit of a compromise, as he would have to move to Los Angeles from the east coast to be with her, but they were talking it over. At any rate, I was excited to see my old roommate again. On my way to where I was meeting them,

If at First (and Second) You Don't Succeed...

I had to pass through the part of town where C and her teammates were competing in their first meet of the season. As I drove, I was acutely aware that C was there, not a mile away. As a result of my own actions, my hands were tied. I wanted more than ever just to look at her—to fully remember and to feel the butterflies she always aroused inside me. But I couldn't. Doing so would only put her feelings at risk, and I wouldn't take that chance.

When I met up with Gina and Daniel, my heart was heavy, but my mood soon picked up. Socializing is often an instant remedy for my emotional ills, if only a temporary fix. I met them at a ritzy restaurant with a bar near the water. Gina was glowing; she had a happiness about her that I am not sure I had ever seen. I cared about her a lot by then, so I was thrilled to see her in such high spirits. Daniel looked the same as I had remembered, and I couldn't help but laugh out loud when I saw him for the first time in four years. Some of Gina's other friends were there as well. I had met one of them before. Her name was Jane, and she lived in the apartment across from Gina's. The others were new to me, but they all seemed to be really nice people. As is usually the case, I spent much of the night answering questions about dental problems. (Just part of being a dentist, I suppose.) Jane and I spent a good deal of time talking at the bar. She seemed to be a really genuine person, and we hit it off well.

Later in the evening, we left the bar and went to a little fifties style café to grab some food for me. The group had eaten dinner earlier, and I had been just a bit late for that, so I needed a little fuel. While we were sitting and socializing, Jane mentioned that she had gone to a gymnastics meet at the local college earlier that evening, just before she came to the restaurant. She had arrived shortly before I had. What a small world. Gina saw my expression change and glared at me admonishingly. Jane happened to notice our little interaction and inquired about it. I was probably too open, but because I am a very trusting person, I figured I could trust Jane. I told her there was a woman that I had an unfortunate history with on the visiting team at the meet she had gone to. We talked about it for a bit, but eventually the subject changed. I didn't tell her too much that time, but she would learn the bulk of the story soon enough.

When I went home that night, I fell right back into turmoil. Questions... What would I do if I quit my job? Could I find another one in the area? Should I start my own practice? Would that be a wise course of action? Should I just move up to LA? How would I get out of my lease if I did that? What about all my bills? Even more distressing were the questions about C. The loss of my mother had reminded me how fragile and fleeting life can be. I didn't want to regret my time in this world, and if I was to live without regrets, I had to do what my heart compelled me to do: I had to keep trying. I wanted her—more than anything I had ever wanted. I wanted to give her everything she needed and so much more. I wanted to show her what real honesty and trust and dedication were all about. I wanted to save her from any possible harm that any dishonest, selfish guy could possibly cause her. But how could I show her without scaring her? Even though it mattered immensely whether or not I actually reached her, I knew that the most important thing to my life and who I was and who I was to become was that I didn't give up. I had to make a stand.

I only worked at my job until the end of the next week. After much contemplation, I decided that I had seen too many discrepancies between the way I wanted to practice dentistry and the way I was being forced to at that practice. I just couldn't ethically continue on. I was ecstatic to be done working there, but I had another problem: lots of expenses and no source of income.

I entertained the idea of opening my own practice after that. I even picked out a practice to buy up in LA County and applied for a loan. The loan was denied, thankfully, because I had no source of income. They say you should never make a big life decision after a major tragedy. With a little time, I decided that the sentiment was correct. Why did I want to open a practice? That would just take more of my time and put me under more stress, while also tying me down for years to come and forcing me to make my living from dentistry. No way did I want that. I had other plans.

If at First (and Second) You Don't Succeed...

I did have to break my lease in Laguna Beach because I couldn't find a job in the area. I wanted to be up in LA anyhow, so I wasn't too disappointed. My landlords were okay with me breaking the lease, as long as they could find someone else to rent from them. I had paid through January, so I stayed until the end of the month and then moved in with Ron and his roommates in one of the coastal cities in LA County. They were cool with me crashing on the couch while I figured out what I was going to do next, and they didn't even charge me any rent. Unfortunately for me, it took two more months after I left my apartment for my landlords to find a new tenant. I tried to find a replacement myself, but in the end, I wound up owing them about five thousand dollars. The tally included two months rent and expenses from trips from Arizona (where they lived) to Laguna Beach to work on finding tenants. It was a crushing blow financially, but I had done what I felt was right by leaving my job, and I was willing to take a larger burden upon myself to make sure I lived ethically. My landlords informed me that I had three months to pay them in full, after which they would charge me ten percent interest per month.

I found a job in LA at the end of January. It was at a small private practice that had been opened over twenty-five years prior; the current owner had purchased it just over three years ago. The office was very nicely decorated and comfortingly lit. Plus, my new boss was a very kind and genuine guy who was very concerned with patient care. I was hired on to work two days per week, and at first, I did. I found out later that patient attendance at the practice could be sporadic, and I was often getting only one day per week or less. That put me in more of a bind financially. I was having a bit of trouble keeping up with paying my debts working two days per week, and it really hurt when I only worked one. I kept looking for another job where I could get a couple more days each week, but there just weren't many openings. For most of the job opportunities I saw, the hiring parties wanted someone with two years of experience. I didn't even have six months yet.

Paige and I had grown closer since my mother's passing, and we had begun to talk on the phone regularly. I couldn't be happier about what we had become. Our friendship was a measure of redemption for a soul that desperately needed it. When I had informed Paige that my mother had died via e-mail, she called and left me a message on my voicemail saying that I shouldn't hesitate to call if I needed someone to talk to. She said she was there for me. It was a sharp contrast from anything most people would have expected after our date. I don't want to overstate the obvious, but we never would have grown to care about each other had I not been persistent in wanting to know her.

39

Life is in the Details

In the face of my worsening financial situation, my heart's unflappable will to pursue C gave me solace. I spent many hours contemplating what I was going to do to reverse my fortunes with her. Ron and I were spending a lot of time with each other, and we had decided to go in on a business venture together. As a result of that, we both read the book *Think and Grow Rich* by Napoleon Hill (1960). It is supposedly a "must read" for any entrepreneur, and I found it very inspiring. The gist of Hill's book is that by "self-suggestion" and an unshakable belief that one will achieve what he or she desires, those desires will become reality. It isn't that this will happen by magic per se, but thoughts lead to actions, and actions lead to results. In some way, the thinking is similar to *The Secret* by Rhonda Byrne (2006), but not quite as mystical (although still a little bit so). *Think and Grow Rich* states that one must be willing to suffer an innumerable amount of defeats without giving up, and that a person must indeed put all their eggs in one basket: no contingency plans—just one goal and no doubt whatsoever that it will come to fruition. More so than applying this to being successful at business, I applied it to C. I wanted to believe those words. I knew I was right for her, more than ever. If I just held to that and didn't give up, maybe she would see it. The book suggested that one should write out a specific statement concerning what he desired, when he wanted it by, and what he was willing to do in return for it; if he read it aloud every night before bed and every morning upon rising, a plan would be revealed to him. If followed, that plan would bring about the desired results. With that in mind, I wrote out a statement about C, and I read it aloud every night and every morning. The idea was that by reading your statement aloud repeatedly, you would start to believe the words. Once you did, the powers that be would reveal a plan to you that would work. It sounds silly, but I needed to believe that somehow, some way, against all odds, and in spite of the mistakes I had made with C in the past, I could still end up with her. Soon after I started my ritual, a plan began to emerge in my mind.

Before my plan took shape, I had an opportunity to take care of some unfinished business. I wanted very much to see C compete at least once, and my chances for that were rapidly disappearing. I had missed her in Los Angeles, and with each passing week, the season came closer to its end. I still didn't have any intention of distracting her, but I figured that I could probably sneak into one of her meets and just hang back, out of sight. She would never know I was there. Which meet though? I didn't have the funds to travel very far or stay in a hotel.

In mid-February, Ron was to make a trip up to San Francisco to meet with some business associates/friends. He had a piece of equipment that he was going to have to transport, but he didn't want to take it on the plane with him because it was very fragile and sensitive. He asked me if I wanted to drive up for the weekend and bring the equipment with me. I thought about it and decided that I could swing it. I loved visiting San Francisco anyhow, and Darren was going to be home for the President's Day weekend. Plus Jeanette (my friend from Veiltown) had recently moved there, and my buddy Scott then lived in the area as well. I could take the opportunity to see three of my very best friends. Then there was the fact that C's team was going to be competing at a school in the area that Sunday afternoon. I could help Ron, visit my friends, and go check out C's meet.

Life is in the Details

I drove up on Friday. Scott lived in a city called Fremont, about an hour from San Francisco. I got there late at night, and we chatted for a few hours before turning in. The next morning, I got up pretty early and headed for San Francisco. I was to stay with Jeanette for the next two nights, and we spent the day together. The two of us walked around some nice spots and talked things over. When lunchtime came, we ate at a quaint little café. There, I told Jeanette about how I was going to go to the gymnastics meet the next day. I had shared some of my story with her while we were in Veiltown and when she had visited me in Orange County in December. She knew all of the basics, for sure. When I told her about the meet, she thought I was nuts: "What? Are you crazy? She's going to think you are stalking her!" I replied, "But I'm not... Besides, I don't plan on letting her see me. I just want to see her compete. That's all." It perplexes me how women in this day and age jump to the "stalker" conclusion so quickly. If a guy has a persistent woman chasing him, he is usually just somewhat annoyed by it, but he seldom makes assumptions that she could be dangerous, unless she actually does something dangerous. Jeanette wasn't saying that she thought I was a stalker, but she did believe that C would think I was if I persisted. I asked her if that was a fair thing to think about someone. She said no, but explained that she knew how women's minds worked and that she would instinctively react that way, given similar circumstances. I bristled at that. "Why? How could you say something so pervasive about someone without actually getting to know him first? You know me! You know I would never hurt her or any woman." She replied, "But SHE doesn't know you! I'm not saying it is the right thing for her to think, but I am saying that she will if you don't leave her alone." She also asked me how I could feel that way about someone I didn't know. "That's like something that I felt when I was in high school!" she said. Thanks for being a killjoy, Jeanette. That conversation put a lot of doubt into my mind, and I started to rethink everything, once again. She was right, or at least she had a good grasp of the risks involved. But I knew the risks. I always had. They just weren't good enough reasons for me to give up.

I met up with Ron and his buddy Will later in the day and gave them the piece of equipment. They popped it in Will's car and took off. Then, I went to Darren's parents' house to meet up with my rapping partner. I hadn't seen him since I left Veiltown, and I broke into a wide smile when he came out to meet me in front of the house. We met up with a group of his old friends from around the area that evening, at one of their apartments. They were good folks, as I expected. We played Nintendo Wii for a few hours and then went to this crazy nightclub that was something like a circus from hell, complete with demons, flaming arrows, and a human sound machine wearing a fuzzy turquoise shirt. It was nuts! All in all, I had a good time. I got back to Jeanette's place at around three o'clock in the morning.

The next day, I awoke and got ready to go to C's gymnastics meet. I made sure I looked my best. I didn't plan on her seeing me, but if she did by chance, it wouldn't hurt to look respectable. I knew that I would be easier to recognize if I didn't wear something to cover up my head. (Not too many people have an appearance like mine.) Before I went to the meet, I headed downtown on the bus and looked for a hat shop. In the end, I purchased a tan Kangol baseball cap. I headed back to Jeanette's place, picked up my car, and drove to the meet.

When I got to the campus, I parked my car and walked to the athletics pavilion. I was nervous that I would be recognized as I made my way into the building, so I looked down as I walked. Once inside, I bought a ticket and tried to figure out where I was going to watch from. As I was walking around the outside of the seating areas, the introductions started. I entertained the idea of sneaking in while they were going on and sitting in the crowd somewhere, but I felt like I would be just a bit too conspicuous. While I was deciding where to go, I heard the announcer say C's name. Hearing it made me smile for a second. Only the first two levels of the stadium were open, but I found an elevator and went up to the third level. The halls were empty there, so I felt a little bit more at ease. I tried to find a spot where I could see all of the areas of the floor where the events were to be held. At the same time, I tried to avoid being in view of the area where C's team had its bench. I thought I had found a spot while the announcer was introducing the other team; it was in the corner of the stadium, behind where C's team was lined up on the floor for introductions. I stood by the railing there, in the shadows, so as to conceal myself the best I could. As I looked out at the floor, I saw her. There she was… just a few hundred feet away from me. Like I said before, I would know her anywhere. As I took her in and my eyes moved over her neck and hair, with its dark roots underneath a bleached blonde exterior, I felt exactly the same as I always had: nervous, excited, shy… The familiarity of those old feelings was comforting, and they reminded me how just being near her was one of the most disarming experiences I could imagine. At that moment, all the hesitation that Jeanette had put into my mind the day before vanished. Whatever the cost, I would try again.

A few seconds passed, and C turned her head to the right. At that moment, I realized that if she were to keep turning around, she would see me. I panicked and sort of fell backwards to avoid being caught in her line of sight. I couldn't stay there, so I went back out into the hall and looked for a new spot. I ended up on the opposite side of the stadium in the corner there. I was right behind C's bench but not visible from it. I could see the entire floor from my vantage point while also being very difficult to see, standing behind the handrails that led up to the next level.

The meet started soon after that, and C's team began the competition on the uneven parallel bars. C had injured her ankle a few weeks before and actually missed an entire meet. She was to only attempt the bars and possibly the balance beam that day. Soon, she came up for her turn. The bars had always been my favorite event in women's gymnastics. If I only got to see C perform on them just once, it would be enough. She began her routine. She was… spectacular. As she spun and flipped and flew through the air, I was hypnotized. Any risk I had taken by coming to the meet had been rewarded right then. She was even more graceful than I remembered. When she prepared to dismount, I held my breath, knowing that a dismount with a sprained ankle is very difficult, if not impossible to land.

She flipped up high into the air and came down hard. As her feet hit, her ankle buckled under the pressure and her leg reflexively stepped to the side to prevent her from falling. She gathered herself and pulled her leg back in to take the proper landing pose. As she did, I let out a long sigh. C's teammates rushed out to congratulate her, and they helped her limp off the mat. I could see in her body language that she was disappointed. Everything except the landing had been flawless. The judges rewarded her with a very high score, but I knew that she wanted to be perfect. I don't suppose that it would have helped her to know that she was perfect, if only in my eyes.

I didn't figure that C would be competing in anything else after that, but I waited around to see. The other team finished their rotation on the bars, and none of them had scored as well as C did. Also, just one of C's teammates had scored higher than her. Her teammate had stuck her landing. If C hadn't stepped out of her landing, she would have easily won the event. I was happy for her. She had done amazingly well, considering her injury, and I hoped that she took some solace in that fact. While I was watching the other girls do their thing, I got a call from Ansel. I had tried to reach him earlier in the day, and he was returning my call. He knew about what I had been through with C and had been very supportive. He asked me what I was doing, and I jokingly said, "Stalking!" We laughed pretty hard for a minute about it. If I only knew then what I know now.

As both teams were preparing to start the last rotation, I watched to see if C was going to give it a go on the balance beam. She walked out from the bench area with her sweat suit jacket on and a towel around her neck. I knew then that she was done for the day. I don't know what came over me at that moment, but I felt very brave. (It was probably stupidity masquerading as courage.) I was sure that when I had sent those e-mails to Sally, she had let C read them; it only seemed logical. Now that I couldn't distract C from competing anymore, I wondered: "What if the letters I sent to Sally had some slow-working affect on her? What if she IS starting to feel differently about me? Maybe just knowing a little more about how she affected me has changed her." I took a chance. I

220

repositioned myself across the tunnel and leaned against the wall, in plain view of the spot where C was standing and watching her teammates warm up for the beam. If she were to look up, she would be able to see me. Whether or not she would recognize me was another issue. I wanted to find out though, and I wanted to see what her reaction would be. It didn't take long. As I stood there, watching her, I noticed that her eyes began to flit around the stadium. They scanned past me, but a second later, returned to where I was standing. I noticed that she was shaking her head, as if saying "no" at one point. It took me a second, but then I realized that someone was standing next to her talking. I hadn't even seen the person approach. At first, I thought C was shaking her head at me, and she may have been. When I saw the other person, I was relieved. I looked away for a few moments and focused on the other girls warming up on the balance beam. Then I looked back at C. It still seemed that she was looking at me (maybe I'm wrong). The person she was talking to had walked away, and there she stood, apparently watching me. I have to admit that the idea of having her attention again, for any possible reason, felt good. I turned away again and waited a few more moments. When I looked back, she was still looking. Was she trying to figure me out? Did she have any idea it was me? It was about time for me to make my exit. I locked my eyes onto C's for a short moment (just to let her know that I knew she saw me), then I turned quickly, pushed myself off from the wall, and headed out through the tunnel. I made haste to my car and drove back to Jeanette's.

I met up with Ron, Will, and another friend/associate of Ron's named Monica that night. We went to a club and danced for a few hours to some reggae. My heart was hopeful, and that made the night a lot of fun. I figured that C would have been frightened and turned away if she thought I was there to hurt her. Maybe she would have even gone and alerted security (not that she needed to). She didn't; she just looked at me. Maybe she was trying to show me that she wasn't afraid of me. At the time, I felt like it was a good sign. Maybe the words of my letter to Sally HAD changed C's mind. Maybe she WAS starting to realize that I was so much more than she had given me credit for. Only time would tell, but I had to get back to LA and start making things happen.

The next day, I said goodbye to Jeanette and headed for Darren's parents' house again. His father was remodeling the kitchen, and I got recruited to help move a gargantuan baker's oven into its permanent position. I got to meet Darren's parents for the first time that day. His sister and brother, whom I had met when they visited Veiltown the year before, were also there. I liked his parents immediately. They were nothing less than the kind of people I would have expected to raise such a great friend. Darren, his father, and I ate at this hamburger joint near their home. Darren had proclaimed the establishment to have "the best burger" he had ever tasted. It was pretty good, I must admit. At the end of the day, I picked up Ron's equipment from Monica's house and headed for Scott's apartment in Fremont. I stayed the night there and headed for home the next day.

During the drive home, I was struck with inspiration. I was having an overflow of emotion, and little thoughts and lines started just sort of popping out of me. I didn't have any paper to speak of, so I used an already-written-on sticky note. I wrote everything I could think of in a square around the address and on the other side, even into the sticky part. When I got home, I would put some structure to it.

I knew from her online bio that C's birthday was at the end of March. I decided that I should give her a gift—but not just any gift. It would have to be a grand and unforgettable gift. Since her college career as a gymnast would be over in April, I thought that it would be nice to give her something recognizing her time at the university. There were a bunch of photos of her competing that were available online, and I had found one very nice picture of her face. (Please remember that it doesn't take any effort at all to find pictures of collegiate athletes on the Internet. All you have to do is type their name into a search engine and press enter.) I decided that I should find an artist to make a sort of a collage of some of those pictures. I also wanted to put her favorite quote into the picture somehow. Like many of the things I knew about C, I knew her favorite quote from her online bio. The quote read: *"Our lives are not determined by what happens to us, but by how we react to what happens; not by what life brings to us, but by the attitude we bring to life. A positive attitude causes a chain reaction of positive thoughts, events, and outcomes. It is a catalyst... a spark that leads to extraordinary results."* I hoped that integrating the quote would make the picture personal to her, and just that much more special.

I didn't have C's address, nor did I have any interest in finding it out. I didn't have the right. Looking up her e-mail address was one thing, but figuring out where she lived without her permission was a line I wouldn't cross. Instead of sending the picture directly to her, I was sure that I could somehow get it to her through the athletics department at the university. She could pick it up there.

At first, I was thinking I could have someone draw the picture. I didn't know how to go about finding an artist to do that though, so I started asking friends for suggestions. DJ said I should try Downtown Disney, which is an outdoor shopping center that is connected to Disneyland. He remembered that when he had been there the year before, there were booths where you could get drawings of yourself made on the spot by artists. He figured that the artists could probably help me out, so I went down and checked it out.

I talked to a guy at one of the booths and told him what I wanted. He thought he could do it, but he would have to run it by his boss. Any work that the artists got through the booth had to be reported to Disney, and a portion of the profit had to be paid to them as well; it was just part of doing business. He gave me his cell number, and I told him I would call him later in the week. I wanted to come back down with a picture of C for him to draw, so I could see if I liked what he could do. After I left the booth, I decided to take a walk around.

Downtown Disney had a fun, energetic atmosphere that night. It was dusk, and there were lots of musicians and such performing up and down the promenade. Families and couples and friends passed by as I headed further away from the parking lot towards Disneyland itself. I felt optimistic. I was taking steps towards something I wanted with all of my being, and that reality was uplifting. I smiled to myself as I imagined C and I there together, walking and holding hands on a warm summer's night. It was still very clear to my logical mind that success was unlikely, but more and more, the belief that I could make her change her mind was growing in my heart. I could turn it around; I just had to believe it. Before my dream could become a reality though, there was still much to be done.

Every morning and every night, I kept reading the statement I had written out about C. More and more I gave myself over to believing it, and as each day passed, my plan changed in proportion to my growing belief. I started to think that maybe the drawing wouldn't be enough. It would be a nice gesture, for sure, but I felt like it wouldn't explain where I was coming from well enough for her to truly understand. As a result, I started to come up with more things I could send her along with it. I like to sing, and my natural voice is decent (if not very polished). With that in mind, I considered sending a recording of me singing a song with the drawing. I have always been very shy about my singing voice. In fact, at that point in time, I had never wanted to sing to any woman at all. Mara used to ask me to sing to her, but I seldom did, and I always felt very self-conscious doing it. It was more stressful to me than anything else. Remarkably, I wanted to sing to C. I wanted to show her as much of me as I could—to share with her things that I wouldn't share with anyone else. I picked out a song that would express my regrets for the way I had interacted with her when we first met: "My Stupid Mouth," by John Mayer(2001). It's a song about a guy who says all the wrong things at a dinner date and messes up any chance he has at getting to know the woman he's with. I could relate. True, I did say that I didn't speak much during our date, but when I did, I said some things that I just shouldn't have. For example, I told C that I had been having trouble sleeping until I got a hold of her earlier in the week. Then I slept much better. That wasn't too forward or anything, right? Then I told her that I had been uneasy about the fact that I was so much older than her, but eventually it just didn't matter anymore because I was so attracted to her. Those aren't things you tell someone on the first date. I had wanted to be guarded, but I was an open book. My attempts to hide the way I felt really just made me look lost and unconfident, as I said before. I guess it was the truth, at the time. There was no time to worry about mistakes. I just had to fix them. She would understand. Brendan (from dental school) had also moved to Southern California and was doing dentistry in Santa Barbara, about two hours north. He had been playing guitar since he was twelve and was quite good at it. He had even performed at the dental school talent show every year we were there, each time to be thanked with loud applause. I explained the story to Brendan and asked him if he would play the guitar for me and help me get the song recorded so I could send it to her. He agreed, and we got to work.

Unlike anything I had ever experienced before, my interactions with C and my feelings for her had unlocked my artistic side. According to my English teachers, I was always pretty good at expression in the medium of writing, but I never had any love for it. I had been praised for my writing in almost every English class I had ever taken, especially since high school began, but I never thought about writing as a hobby until I started working on my project in Idaho after school ended. At the same time, I started writing poetry. Guess what the subject was. I wrote two poems as I waited for my license. They weren't that great, but they were a start. After I finished my project in December, I had not written anything else for while. Once I began my trip home from San Francisco, ideas seemed to flow freely from inside of me. I guess in a way, C was my muse. I wrote seven poems about her in the next few weeks. They were all much better than the first two had been, and that made me go back and clean those two up a bit. In particular, two of the new ones were better than the rest. One was an extremely long quatrain, and the other was in free verse. The free verse poem was the one I had started writing on my way back from San Francisco. As I was writing the last few verses of it, it dawned on me that I should send it to C. It was the most artistic and beautiful thing that had ever come out of me, and it was C who inspired it. She should have it; it was hers. And if she chose to look, it would help her see why I was worth her time.

As I practiced singing John Mayer's song to get my voice ready for recording, I decided that I should write a song for C and send her a recording of that too. It wouldn't be too hard to do. I had been listening to John Mayer's newest album quite a bit at the time, and it was basically all blues. Under that influence, I wrote some blues lyrics and had Brendan compose me some music. I called the song "Sunshine." Although not an original thought, it was my first real attempt at writing a song, and I was pretty happy with it. I hoped she would be too.

The artist from Downtown Disney and I met up at his booth again about a week after the first time we met. I gave him a picture of C that I had gotten off the Internet, and he took it home, drew a sketch of it, and sent it to me over e-mail. I didn't really like it. It wasn't as realistic as I wanted it to be, but I figured he could do better if I just gave him more instruction on what I was looking for. Frustratingly, after he sent me the sketch, I had trouble getting hold of him again. Eventually, I talked to the owner of the booth and he couldn't locate him either. I hoped that he was alright, but his disappearance put me in a dilemma. I needed to find an artist who could do what I wanted and quickly. Time was ticking away. The owner of the booth was disappointed in his employee, and he didn't want me to suffer because of his disappearance, so he gave me the name of an artist he knew that he believed could do the job. I called him as soon as I could, and after I explained what I was trying to get done, he told me that he didn't think his talents were suited for it. He gave me another artist's phone number. That artist ended up being the guy.

I met with the artist over coffee at a restaurant in a city in the north part of Orange County. Gary was a professional who worked in just about every medium. He suggested that he should do the picture in watercolor, as in his experience, it would be the best medium for this sort of thing. He quoted me a price, and I had to think about it for a few moments. It was quite a bit more than I had wanted to pay, but it was fair. From the looks of some of the photos he had shown me of works he had done with the same sort of structure, I was certain that the result would be good. I really wasn't in a position to pay as much as he asked, but C was more of a priority to me than anything had ever been, so I figured, "What the hell…" We made a deal, and I sent Gary the pictures of C that I wanted him to use. He got on it immediately.

At that point, I was going to send C a painting, a poem, and two songs on CD. I still didn't feel like I had enough though. I felt like I had to explain more to her, just to make sure that she got it. I wrote her another letter. I poured my heart out into that Microsoft Word document. I didn't want to send her a piece of paper to read though. I wanted her to hear me speak the words the way that I wrote them—with emotion. I decided to record myself reading the letter over an appropriate instrumental, and include it on the CD after the two songs. I could add it on when Brendan and I made the final copy. Once I decided on that, I figured that my feelings would be explained fully by all of the things that I would send. One more thing remained though. I wanted to put my face to the gifts. She needed to be able to connect it all to me somehow, and maybe a picture of me would give her a way to do that. I didn't want to send her a picture of me smiling or something like that. It would come off as crass, as far as I was concerned. I wanted the picture, like everything else I would send her, to make a statement: to show her who I was and what I was about. I had a perfect idea, thanks to my photographer friend Lana. (I mentioned her for a brief moment earlier.) She had a picture of her taken where she was sitting on the ground without a shirt, her arms strategically placed to cover her… shame. Across the spot where her heart would be, she had a red X, and her face showed a forlorn expression. It was a beautiful piece of art. I decided that I would have Lana take a picture of me wearing an unbuttoned purple shirt. With my left hand, I would pull the top of the shirt back to reveal a red X over the spot where my heart would be. With my right hand, I would hold a red heart. On the heart would be C's name, written in white. I would extend the heart forward as if to say, "Take it… It belongs to you."

Paige and I were talking frequently at that point. I had spent a lot of effort building a friendship with her, and things were going nicely, but I didn't want to take a chance of destroying it all by telling her about C and that whole situation. What if she didn't understand? We just talked about other things. I still hoped she would move to LA because I wanted us to be able to hang out as friends, now that we were comfortable with each other. I also thought it was a chance for her to get outside of her comfort zone. Judging by the way her life was going at the time, she could have used a little risk. I tried to nudge her forward as much as I could, but she was still mulling it over.

I have mentioned before that when Paige and I became friends, I felt extremely validated. During one conversation with her, about three weeks before C's birthday, I got an even bigger ego boost. We were talking about a guy that she had been dating, and somehow, we got to a point in the conversation where she said this to me: "I think that when you and I met, the timing was just off." I knew what she was getting at, so I jumped all over it: "Wait a minute! If I remember correctly, you didn't want anything to do with me after our date." She replied, "I didn't." I asked, "What do you mean then? I'm not sure I understand." To that she said, "Well, I didn't know what a great personality you had." I just laughed out loud. See?! This wonderful woman who had written me off on a first impression had just admitted to me that she had thought about me in a romantic way, at least in some capacity. I was flattered, of course. The great thing about it was that nothing changed after Paige told me that. She really had deep feelings for the guy she was dating then, and I was all wound up over C, so we just kept on being friends. However, discovering that fact made me hopeful about the endeavor that I was undertaking. A few weeks later, I felt it was safe to trust Paige with all of the details about my pursuit of C. She was supportive and kind, and we talked it over for a few hours.

40

Careful Who You Trust

In middle of all of this, I made a terrible mistake. Like I said before, I am a very trusting person; and in spite of the fact that being so trusting has burned me many times before, I have continued to be trusting. I think I finally learned my lesson though, because I misplaced my trust so badly that it caused me to lose a friend.

I was still spending time with Gina every other week or so at that point. I had even helped her move into the condo she had just purchased, spending an entire Saturday with her and staying over for the night. After I had sent the e-mail to Sally in November, Gina had been very clear about her feelings that I shouldn't continue to pursue anything with C. We had talked about it, and she told me that if she were to end up in a similar situation with a persistent man, she would be frightened. She, like Jeanette, thought that if I did any more, I would look like a stalker. Of course... When I decided to try again, I didn't share that fact with Gina. I knew she wouldn't understand or approve, and I didn't want to argue about it or put a strain on our still growing friendship.

Jane was moving in with Gina at her new condo. The reason they were both moving was that their building was to be torn down and all the tenants had to find new places to live. Jane and I had started to become friends as well, and I helped her get her stuff organized at the condo on Sunday of the weekend after I helped Gina move. We talked a lot that day, and I felt secure that I could reveal more about the gymnast and my scars. I explained all that had happened and she really seemed to understand where I was coming from. I also asked her not to talk to Gina about any of it, because she would be upset at me for continuing to hang onto it. I thought that sharing with Jane would make us closer. Once I had finally figured out everything that I was going to send C, I told Jane about it on the phone one day. She was supportive and wished me luck. I thought it reflected well on her that she was able to be so kind and respectful of what I had to do. She was even encouraging.

The next day, Gina and I had planned to get together and eat dinner after I got off work. When I checked my e-mail in the morning, I had a letter from her in my inbox. I opened it, thinking she was just checking in or adjusting the plans a bit. What she was actually doing made me instantaneously sick to my stomach. The letter read something like this:

Darren,

This thing with C is really getting scary. I am sorry, but I have to take a step back from our relationship at the moment. I hope that isn't hurtful. I wish you luck in your future.

Gina

Instantly, I thought of Jane: "How could she?! I trusted her!" I e-mailed Gina back, pleading with her not to end our friendship. I told her that I really needed her support at the moment and that it would make me really sad to lose what we had, especially after we had been able to get over our sordid past. She wouldn't listen. She wrote back and told me that she wouldn't change her mind. I replied by telling her that if she chose to close the door on me now, I hoped that she would someday choose to reopen it. In the blink of an eye, one of the most comforting and best parts of my current life had vanished. It made me feel horrible. I tried to contact Jane as well, although I didn't do it in anger. I just wanted to talk it over with her. Truthfully, I did understand what they both thought of me, to some extent, and I wanted to show Jane that it was unfounded. I wasn't a danger to C or to anyone else. Sadly, Jane didn't respond to my attempts to contact her. Perception had its way with me once again. Evidently, most women will perceive a guy who doesn't give up as dangerous, even when he couldn't be further from it.

I told DJ what had happened, and he was miffed. He asked me what I thought the whole occurrence indicated about the kind of person Gina was. It seemed to me that it indicated some pretty bad things, but I didn't see any value in blaming her for being a rotten person. I wanted to be her friend, and now I couldn't. As much as she hurt me by abandoning me when I really needed her, I know that she had her reasons. I was willing to accept them, even if she couldn't accept my own. I tried to put it all behind me, even though it saddened me immensely and also delivered a massive, damaging blow to my conviction. I had to keep going though. I didn't have time to feel sorry for myself. Contrary to what Gina and Jane thought, things could still turn out right.

41

The Home Stretch

DJ and I were talking about all the things I was going to send C over the phone one day, and he had a great suggestion. He thought that I should tie it all together somehow—give it a theme. That got me thinking. I wanted to do it, definitely. That would make all of it even more creative and more likely to strike a chord with C. I came up with this: I would wrap each item separately and put it all inside of a box. On each item, there would be an envelope with a number from one to four on it, indicating in what order she should open the items. The first envelope would be on the painting. Inside the envelope would be a card that read: "My eyes." The second envelope would be on the CD. The card inside would read: "My voice." The third envelope would be on the picture, and the card inside would read: "My heart." The last envelope would be on the poem. Its card would read: "My soul." How could she deny me after all that?

On the day that I got the friendship-ending letter from Gina, I was reading Yahoo news at work and an article caught my eye. The article was about a little-known digestive disorder called Celiac disease. The author stated that many Americans had the disorder, but did not know it; indeed a large group of people was even misdiagnosed with other digestive ailments because Celiac disease was thought to be so rare. Many doctors didn't even consider it as a possibility, if they knew of it at all. When a person has Celiac disease, he or she cannot eat anything that contains a plant protein called gluten. If gluten is consumed, it causes an immune response at the sites in the small intestine where the gluten is being absorbed. The immune response destroys the gluten as well as the lining of the intestine, thus causing digestive unrest and pain. It also leads to improper absorption of certain nutrients, including calcium. I started to read about the symptoms of the disease, and they seemed to be pretty much the same as the symptoms I had been experiencing since my trouble with C had begun over a year prior. I knew that stress initially had much to do with my ailment, and I had been under a decent bit of stress lately although I felt I was coping much better than I had previously. (I did wonder how my stomach was going to respond to the haymaker that Gina and Jane had hit me with earlier in the day.) The symptoms had gone from very slight to extremely bad since I had first started spending time with Ron. In fact, when I moved in with him, the severity had made a huge jump. I was compelled to figure it out, so I found a website that had a list of foods that contained gluten. As it turned out, wheat, rye, and barley all contained gluten. Gluten was also used as an ingredient in many processed foods (such as salad dressing) to add body, and it was found in some vegetable gums. It also had a few aliases, such as "modified food starch," and "vegetable protein." All those things made me wonder because my diet contained a lot of wheat bread, and I was eating salads regularly. The most alarming fact was that there was wheat in soy sauce. Ron was half Japanese, and since we had become friends, we had been eating a lot of sushi and other soy sauce containing meals. When I moved in with him, I had gotten a good look at his diet and added a lot of elements from it into my own. My digestion had gotten worse than it had ever been. I was hesitant to just stop eating all of those things that I enjoyed so much. What if my problems didn't get any better? Nonetheless, I didn't have any insurance, and spending money on an outrageously expensive visit to the doctor's office wouldn't even be possible with my financial affairs the way they were. (Not to mention the fact that I had put myself under even more monetary duress by undertaking my plan to profess my feelings to C; it was not cheap.) I talked it over with DJ, and soon after, I decided I had no choice but to take gluten out of my diet and see what happened.

I am so glad I stumbled onto that article… Within a week of throwing out and giving away all of my wheat and gluten containing foods, my digestion was markedly better. After two, it was completely back to normal. When I think of the fact that many Americans live with Celiac disease for years with minor symptoms as they unknowingly destroy their digestive tracts, I thank the stars above that I was able discover what my problem was.

You might be thinking that the digestive unrest I experienced while I was in Veiltown probably wasn't due to C at all—just to a poor diet. I thought long and hard about that too. After a lot of consideration, I am still certain that my consternation over C played a major part in it. Autoimmune diseases (where the body's immune system attacks parts of the body) such as Celiac disease are rare, but it has been demonstrated in many cases that stress can elicit the onset of such conditions, including Celiac disease. One example in dentistry is an oral condition called Lichen Planus. I can remember times during high school that I had very minor versions of the same symptoms I experienced before I stopped eating gluten. (Usually those symptoms would arise when I would eat too many cheeseburgers—meaning a whole bunch of bread.) When my life got too stressful for me to effectively cope with, my immune system started to malfunction even more (as immune systems are likely to do during times of stress). That made the response to gluten in my digestive tract increase in intensity. Once the response got out of hand, I became extremely sensitive to gluten. Now, when I eat even a little of it, I feel the effects the next day. That is a rather long-winded explanation, but the take-home message here is that my stress reaction to my situation with C had been so severe that it caused my condition to worsen to a clinically significant level. Once I rid myself of gluten, even in the face of immense stress, my digestive system ceased to suffer. That… was a load off my mind.

As C's birthday approached rapidly, things fell into place. I decided that I didn't want to take the chance of the painting being damaged during shipping, so I bought a plane ticket to fly to Veiltown at the end of March. I was hard-pressed to afford the flight. Notwithstanding that fact, I knew that if I could somehow win the day, any monetary consequences would be more than worth it. I would transport the painting and the CD myself. I could stay with DJ in his apartment and kick it with him, Darren, and some of my other friends for a few days. I would meet up with Lana and have her take the picture. After that, we could get it printed and put it in the package. DJ agreed to take the package to the university's athletics department for me and drop it off with a compliance officer I had been corresponding with. I knew that there would be issues with leaving a birthday gift for C at the athletics department, so I had gotten in touch with the officer ahead of time and gave him a brief, incomplete explanation of what the situation was. He just needed to make sure that it wasn't some sort of expensive booster gift, so I agreed to let him see what was inside the box before it was sealed.

I had the poem set onto a scroll with some graphics in the background, golden finials (the knob type things on the end of a scroll), and red and gold tassels. The place I used was based in New Jersey, and I found them on the Internet. I had the scroll sent to DJ's apartment and he got it about a week before I came up.

I was to pick up the painting just about a week before my plane flight. I met up with Gary at the same restaurant in Orange County, and he gave me the finished product. In all seriousness, I was literally speechless when I saw it for the first time. It was truly stunning. We had decided to put purple matting around it, inside of a gold frame. Centered at the bottom of the matting was the quote. I had told Gary a bit about my story and why I was having this painting commissioned at our previous meeting. He felt for me. When I met him to pick it up, he reduced the price by two hundred dollars. I would have paid an extra two hundred dollars for the piece of art he gave me (and even more), but it was a nice gesture, and it definitely helped me out financially.

That night I told Gary the rest of the story. He listened thoughtfully as I laid it out to him. He understood how I felt, but was hesitant to bless my plan. He just thought it was too much, given the circumstances. He suggested that I give C the painting and a card saying something simple and sweet, but nothing else. He thought that the painting was already as grand of a gesture as I could ever need, and anything more would be overkill. I had been so proud of all the things I came up with to give to C, but after talking to Gary, I started to second-guess myself again. Over the next couple of days, I decided to just do what Gary said. I am truly thankful for his perspective and his advice, but I wonder if I made a mistake by listening to him.

I was to go see Brendan up in Santa Barbara that coming weekend so we could record me speaking the letter and make the final CD. We had worked on the project quite a bit over the previous few weeks, and we had recorded the final versions of the two songs. (We only needed to master them.) After changing my mind, I called Brendan and told him that I wouldn't need the CD after all. Even so, I told him that it had been a blast making music with him and that I hoped we could do more in the future. I also got in touch with Lana and told her that I wouldn't need her to take my picture, but I was looking forward to seeing her anyhow.

Everyone I spent any time talking to about my decision to only give C the painting thinks that I did the right thing by not following through with my original plan. Everyone, that is, except DJ. He thought I was falling back when I needed to push forward. He asked me, "Why not just be who you are? Why not just put it all on the table and let the chips fall where they may?" The answer is: I was scared. I didn't want C to think I was crazy, so I lost my nerve. If I could go back and do it all over again, I would have listened to DJ, simply because of the principle on which he based his opinion. He knows me as well as anyone, and he knows what makes me tick. He thought I should have listened to my heart, instead of everyone else's reasoning. He told me that no one else I knew would have the courage to even try again. Not that it made them any less valuable people or friends, but I was different than everyone else; therefore, I shouldn't do what anyone else would do. "Just be yourself, man." I can see now that even if the results ended up being the same, they would have been that way with me giving everything I had instead of holding back. I would be able to be proud of that. I should have known that out of all the people in the world, DJ would be the one to trust. I'll never make that mistake again.

The time came, and I flew to Veiltown with the paining under my arm, in a box I had to construct myself from pieces of other boxes. It looked professional enough though, so I wasn't concerned with the impression it would make on C. When DJ and I got to his apartment, I got to see the scroll with my poem on it for the first time. Just like the painting, it was beautiful. I wondered if I should have DJ deliver it along with the painting, but decided against it. I hoped that I would get the chance to give it to C in person.

I drove DJ to the athletics administration building the day after I arrived, and he took the painting in and delivered it to the compliance officer. The officer inspected it, and agreed to give it to C. At that point, I could have delivered it myself, but if C happened to be in the building when I was dropping it off, everything could be ruined. I didn't want to chance it, so DJ delivered it for me (the way we had planned). The gymnastics team would be competing at the conference championships in another city that weekend, and I didn't want to distract C from the task at hand, so I had DJ write an instruction on the box: "Don't open until after championship." She could open it afterwards, and I wouldn't feel guilty. With the painting, there was a greeting card. It was yellow with three flowers on the front. On the inside, which was originally blank, I wrote this: "Sometimes we forget... My hope with this gift is that someday, if you need, you can look upon it and remember, not who you were, but who you are. I won't contact you again, but my light will always be on..." At the bottom, I left my phone number. After dropping off the gift, DJ came back outside, and I drove him to his class. It was done. There was no turning back.

Lana came over to meet us the next afternoon. I had let her read the poem over e-mail before, and she wanted to see the way it looked on the scroll. When I showed it to her, she reread the whole thing! She loved it and thought that the scroll made it even that much better. The way she felt about my words was very flattering; after all, she was a true-blue artist. The three of us chatted for a few hours, and then she left. I walked her to her car in the rain and watched her drive off.

The next day, I returned to Los Angeles. I didn't know what was going to happen with C, but I was certain of one thing: all the work I had put into attempting to convince her had been more fulfilling than anything I had done in quite a long time. No matter the outcome, I wouldn't regret trying again. It was what I had to do, no matter the consequences. I was ready to face any repercussions that might come (or so I thought).

42

Rock Bottom

Ron was a member of the Army Reserve, and he had to go away to the east coast to participate in an officer's training course for five months when I got back from Veiltown. He had been considering subletting his room in the house while he was gone, and he offered it to me. I couldn't afford the eight hundred and twenty five dollars each month, but I could barely do about six hundred and fifty. Ron thought it over and decided that having me stay in his room would be a better idea than having some stranger move in, even if he had to pay a little bit of cash for that to happen. He left for Oklahoma the day after I got back from Veiltown, and I moved off the couch and into his bedroom for the next five months. It was nice to sleep in a bed again, but it sucked that Ron had to leave for so long. We had developed a pretty solid friendship over the last few months. I would miss him, for sure.

I waited. C wouldn't get the painting until the next week, when the team got back from the conference championships. I should have kept a positive attitude. It isn't like worrying and being afraid will ever help a person accomplish a daunting task. Regrettably, I started letting my fears take hold of me. Now that the time had come, it just didn't seem like my heart's wishes could come true, no matter how I wanted to believe. All of the doubts that the others had expressed had taken center stage in my heart. I tried to beat them back the best I could, but it just didn't work. The days came and went, and I was having awful trouble sleeping at night against my worries. Then something else disheartening happened. In the first week of April, a man in his forties came onto C's campus and shot his ex-girlfriend to death. He then killed himself. The woman was twenty-six. As it turned out, she had put a restraining order on him, but it didn't stop him from taking her life. When I read the story on the Internet, I immediately feared that the shootings would put C in a bad frame of mind about me and my gift. "Shit! Why did this have to happen now?!" I thought. She had probably opened the painting by then, and the only thing I could think to do was e-mail her and try to assuage her fears. In my letter, I told her that I was aware that I had told her I would not contact her again, but I had just read about the shootings on campus, and I wanted to assure her that I would never ever harm her; I wasn't capable of anything like that. After that, I said goodbye. It was my last goodbye. I hoped that C would believe me and not worry. Sadly, there was no way for me to know how she felt, and that bothered me more than I can explain. I couldn't bear the thought of her lying in her bed at night, thinking I might be lurking in the shadows somewhere, waiting to jump out and attack her. That was so far from reality… but she didn't know that.

After that, my nights became even more restless and tortured. I would think about my mother and Jake and Gina and my growing financial troubles. All of a sudden, absolutely everything was crashing down on me. I couldn't get another job, no matter how hard I looked, and my bills were getting harder and harder to keep up with. I even had to borrow money from my father a couple of times (not that he could afford it either). I wondered how I would get out from under the immense mountain of debt I had accumulated, especially considering that my current state of mind had me feeling like I hated dentistry and didn't want to do it anymore. How would I pay all my expenses then? C hadn't contacted me, and I knew that there was almost no chance that she ever would at that point. To make matters worse, she was probably convinced I was dangerous. I really started to think about where my life was headed, and I came to the realization that I wasn't happy and hadn't been for any extended period since dental school had started almost five years ago. "How did all this happen?" I wondered. I used to know who I was and where I was headed. I used to have direction. I used to have conviction, confidence, love… I could see my future, and it was bright. Now, I just couldn't get my bearings about me. The world seemed to spin around me so fast that I had no chance of righting my ship. No matter how my heart told me to believe I could find my way, every step I took in faith betrayed me. Why should I have believed in anything good? All I did was try to be a better person and to do the right thing and follow my heart, but it was bringing me nothing but anguish. For the first time in my life, I started to lose my will to fight.

Things got so bad in my mind so quickly. As I lay in my bed one night during the second week of April, a thought that had previously been completely unknown to me crept into my mind: "If I can't find a reason to live soon, I should commit suicide. No use existing like this much longer." I didn't want to think that way. Suicide? "No way! Not me." Yet the thought was there: staring into the heart of me, penetrating into all that I was, and somehow, comforting me. I didn't have to suffer anymore. I could end it all. No one would really miss me anyhow. I was just a burden—a fool who couldn't reconcile the demands of reality with what he wanted from life. I had no passion left, except that which I held for C; that passion was to go on unquenched for the rest of my life. Happiness had left me five years ago, never to return.

I didn't tell anyone about how I was feeling except DJ and Darren. They were stunned. When I told DJ, his reaction was, "WHOA WHOA WHOA! What are you talking about? You? Suicide? I never thought I'd see the day!" Darren just breathed in deeply as he searched for something to say. I assured them both that I wasn't anywhere near actually doing it, but if I couldn't figure out a way to bring some happiness back into my life within the next couple of years, I would consider it in earnest. That probably didn't ease their minds much.

43

Lower Still

How can one go lower than rock bottom? I honestly thought that things couldn't get any worse. I had lost my mother, a friend that I had grown to love, and any chance at a future with the most perfect woman I could imagine. I was struggling to pay my bills (even more so after spending all that money on my attempt at winning C's heart), and I needed to find more work in a field that I didn't want to be in. I was a zombie. I hated waking up on the mornings that I actually had to work. All I wanted to do was go to the gym and hang around the house. The fact that I still desired to exercise was somewhat encouraging; it showed me that I hadn't become utterly despondent, at the very least. But I was still so listless. I was just going through the motions each day. I hoped and prayed that things would somehow get better, but I was convinced that the chances of that were slim. To make matters worse, Paige decided that instead of moving to LA, she was going to move to Hawaii to be with the guy she was dating. Then, she basically cut off communication with me without a very good explanation. It was disheartening to lose her that way, but I was used to pain by then. What was one more disappointment?

Early in the month, Rachelle told me that one of the practices that her boss owned needed an associate dentist for Thursdays. Even though the last thing I wanted at that point was to do more dentistry, I absolutely had to take the opportunity to see if I could land the job. The practice was in downtown LA. I interviewed with the owner, and she liked me enough to give me a "working interview" (meaning I would work for a day and she would evaluate me) at the end of the second week of April. I worked my day and she decided to hire me. I would make more money per day than I was making at the other practice, and the patient flow was steadier, so it would help me out financially quite a bit. My first official day of work was to be Thursday, the nineteenth of April.

I had bought a used car right before I left to deliver the painting to DJ in Veiltown. I had driven my old Honda Civic hatchback since I was a senior in high school; my dad bought it for me on my birthday because I had a good senior year, as far as grades went. It was a great car for eleven years, but it was starting to die, and I knew that there was no cost-effective way to save it. The registration was to expire at the end of March, so I had to bite the bullet and buy another car. It was a 2001 Toyota Camry sedan, and I got it from a used car dealership for eight thousand dollars. (Obviously, I didn't have that much cash, so I financed it.) I didn't have time to get the car checked out before I bought it because of the impending trip to Veiltown. However, it ran well, so I trusted that the folks at the dealership were honest. (HA!) When I got back from Veiltown and took it to a mechanic to get it checked out, the car had a bunch of problems. I won't bore you with the details, but the dealership was not cooperative about fixing most of the things that were out of whack. To fix every problem that the dealership refused to, it would cost me over sixteen hundred dollars—a price that I could not pay at the moment. Fortunately, none of the problems were catastrophic, so I decided to get them fixed in order of importance, as I could afford it.

On the night of April eighteenth, I actually got to sleep early for me: by nine o'clock. I was exhausted from all of my emotional troubles, as well as working that day. Even my habitual insomnia couldn't prevent me from falling asleep that night. At ten-thirty PM, a ringing sound ripped me out of my slumber. I groggily grabbed for the phone and tried hard to focus as I read the caller ID. It was DJ. "Dammit! What does he want?" When I answered, I could tell right away that he was worried. In a low and concerned voice he told me that he had been watching TV a second ago, and a commercial for the evening news at eleven had come on. The story that they were leading with was about some complaints filed with the university police that someone was stalking the women's gymnastics team. I completely lost my breath. "Did she?! Really?! No!!!" DJ said he hadn't seen the news report yet, but he told me he would call me when he did and let me know if they were talking about me. I sat in bed stunned and barely able to breathe for the next forty minutes, just praying my heart out that the news report wasn't about me. When DJ called back, he informed me that my worst fear had come true: I was the stalker. "Stalker…" But it wasn't just me. Evidently, some other person had been calling some of the team members on their cell phones, telling them that he had seen them in various places and describing to them what they had been wearing. When they spoke about me, they just said that on Monday, a twenty-two year old team member had reported receiving several e-mails from a twenty-nine year old man who lived in California. They didn't say my name (thank God!), but all doubt had been eliminated from my mind. It was definitely me. There was even speculation that the person making the phone calls and the man in California were the same person! What evidence was there of that? DJ directed me to two newspaper articles he had found online about the case. I let him go and went to the computer to read the articles. One was very unprofessional and biased, in fact calling me a "stalker." The first part of the paragraph focusing on me started out with something to the effect of: "In the case of another woman, the stalker is e-mailing his victim." What happened to "innocent until proven guilty?" The other article was somewhat more unbiased, but still didn't paint me in a very favorable light. There was so much more to all of this, and no one would ever know my side of it.

Needless to say, my night of sleep was destroyed. My stomach was in knots. I had to wait for the morning to come so I could call the campus police department and tell them whatever they wanted to know. In the mean time, I panicked and started destroying everything that had anything to do with C. I deleted all the e-mails I had saved from our correspondence the year before and all of the poems I had written about her from my hard drive; I also shredded the floppy disks that I had backed them up on. I deleted the letters I had written to her but never sent, and I deleted any e-mails to or from friends in which anything about C was mentioned (including an e-mail from Gary containing a scan of the painting). Lastly, I took the statement about C that I had been reading aloud every morning and night and shredded it too. I couldn't believe that I had ever bought into that crap. So much for the power of positive thinking. I took the shreddings from the shredder and threw them in the garbage can with the rest of the trash that would be picked up in the morning. The only thing I kept was the scroll. There was no way anyone could specifically determine that I had written it for C by looking at it, and I was still very proud of it, so I kept it. I had hung it on the wall and left it there since I had been back from Veiltown. I took it down, put it back into its tube, and hid it in the closet.

I don't know what I was thinking. I half expected a S.W.A.T. team to burst into the house and pin me to the floor while searching through my belongings and confiscating anything that could be used as evidence. That didn't happen, but if it would have, they wouldn't have found much (well… at least until they picked through my hard drive and recovered the data). By the time I was all done destroying things, my stomach hurt intensely and I felt nauseated and light-headed. I tried to lie down, but it didn't help because inside my mind, pandemonium was breaking loose. "I'm not a stalker! What if my name gets out? What if someone prints it in the school paper?" I thought. Even if I could sue and win for libel, the repercussions that would have on my reputation could be disastrous. What if I couldn't get a job because of it? There wasn't a doubt in my mind that this episode would come up somehow. If it did, I would most likely suffer severe consequences because even though I wasn't a criminal, the court of public opinion would probably not be very forgiving of my mistakes. At the very least, I would have to explain myself, and that didn't sound like much fun.

I knew that there was some possibility that things would come to the place they ended up as I continued to push, but I honestly didn't think it would happen. C was too smart to think such a ridiculous thing about me. She was too kind. I had hoped that she would be able to just accept the painting, even if she still didn't want to give me a chance to know her. Maybe if she could appreciate the gift (if certain things happened later on), she might even seek me out eventually. A fool's hopes, I know... Things were as clear as they were going to get now. I had scared her: enough for her to go to the police. Maybe if my timing was better, this wouldn't have happened. There was the shooting on campus two weeks before, the guy who had been calling the girls on the team, and on top of all that, there had been another college campus shooting on Monday of that week. I'm not sure whether or not C had reported me after the story showed up on the news, or if it influenced her to do so in any way, but I knew that it couldn't have eased her mind any (especially considering that the guy in the second shooting had been accused of stalking two women previously). Whatever the case may have been, there I was, having been reported to the police for stalking C. I couldn't help but feel that e-mailing her had been a mistake. I should have just kept my word and left her alone. That's what I got for caring about someone who didn't want to know me, much less care about me.

After running circles in my mind for around twenty minutes, I decided that I needed to get out of the house. I got in my car and drove to the freeway. I rolled down the windows and let the engine loose, trying to find some clarity in the wind that whipped into the cabin. There was none—only fear and worry. I drove around for an hour or so, then headed for home feeling no better than I had when I left, and probably worse. On my way, I noticed that my gas tank was very low and I would need to refill it. I stopped near the house to get gas. When I turned the car off, I heard a sort of gurgling sound coming from the engine.

"What is that?" I thought. I had never heard a car make that sound before. Then I noticed that the temperature gauge was showing that the car was extremely hot. I got out and opened up the hood to see if I could determine the cause of the noise. The radiator had a small bit of steam leaking out of it at its cap. I kicked it open, knowing full well that grabbing the cap with my hand would lead to severe burns. As it released, a whole bunch of steam rushed out into the surrounding air. I waited for that to stop, and then I took a bunch of paper towels and grabbed the cap. I turned it a quarter turn, released it, and ran for my life. The cap shot up into the air about thirty feet and plummeted to the concrete. It was followed by a cascade of water that doused the ground all around the front of the car. My radiator was full of water… WATER! I stood there in front of the car, looking up at the sky and laughing hysterically. My laugh turned into a yell of utter frustration at its tail end. Was there something else that could go wrong? I guess making sure that the proper fluids were in the cars they sold didn't fall under the "important" section of this dealership's responsibilities list. (You can put water in a radiator in today's cars, but they are designed to use antifreeze/coolant. Water won't work for very long at all.) What was next with this car?! Milk in the transmission? Peanut butter in the oil pan? I waited for the car to cool down as I filled it with gasoline. Then, I got out the bottle of antifreeze/coolant I had in my trunk and poured what was left of it into the radiator. I only had about half a bottle, so when I started driving, the car began to overheat almost immediately. Luckily, the supermarket wasn't far, and I was able to make it there before the car locked up on me. I bought a couple of bottles of coolant and filled the radiator. Afterwards, I waited a while so the car could cool down some more, then I drove home.

By the time I got home and cleaned myself up, it was three-thirty in the morning. If I could have fallen asleep at that point, it is possible that I could have gotten up and been at work by nine o'clock. Messing with the car had been a temporary reprieve (if not an infuriating one). Now that I was certain that the problem was fixed, I went right back to worrying. I didn't fall asleep until six-thirty AM. I knew that I wasn't going to my new job at that point and that I was going to lose it. It just kept piling on…

I awoke at eight AM with my stomach still churning and called my new (and soon to be former) place of employment. The owner didn't understand why I couldn't come in. I didn't want to tell her what had really happened, but I told her that I had a real, honest emergency and that I had to take care of it. I also told her that I had been up all night dealing with it, which was true. She fired me right there, but I expected as much. I felt bad because Rachelle had gotten me that job and I didn't want to let her down by making her look bad. I couldn't do anything about it at that point. It just was what it was.

Next, I called the university police at C's school and asked to speak with the officer who the papers had quoted about the stalking case. When he came on the line, I told him my name and asked him if he knew who I was. He told me that he thought he did and asked me to hold on for a second, presumably so he could start recording the call or at least to get a pen and pad to jot down what I said. When he got back on the line, I explained my side of the story to him and what exactly I had done. He was aware of the painting and the e-mail I had sent to C already. I apologized to him and assured him that I meant no harm with my actions. I just wanted to do something special for C; that was all. He was quick to tell me that he understood and that I didn't need to worry. From what he had seen, I hadn't done anything illegal; I hadn't made any threats or physically harmed anyone. He thought that my timing was just bad because of the two recent shootings. "People are a bit on edge at the moment," he said. I was relieved to find that he was able to be impartial and not jump to conclusions. I just wish the media had been as prudent. The officer told me that he would have the detective assigned to the case call me within the next few minutes; she would officially question me. I agreed, and we hung up.

The detective called me about ten minutes later, and she asked me a few questions. She asked if it was true that I had been in Veiltown recently, and I told her that it was. I explained that I didn't want the painting that I was going to have delivered to C damaged in shipping, as it was somewhat expensive. I also explained that I had gone to dental school at the university and that I was visiting friends while I was in Veiltown. She seemed satisfied with that and didn't ask me too much more, but she told me that C had told her that she just wanted me to stop contacting her. I was a little indignant at that, and I told the detective that I had told C very clearly that I wouldn't contact her again. I had gone back on what I said because of the shootings on campus, but only so that I could assure C that she wasn't in any danger. At any rate, C was going to come in that afternoon and give the detective her official report. The detective said she would call me if she had any more questions. I asked her if she could do me a favor before we got off the phone; I asked her to tell C that I was really, really sorry. She told me she would relay the message.

What would happen now? I worried for weeks that my name would get out on the Internet, and soon, the whole world would think I was a stalker. Every day, I would search for articles having to do with the episode. The school's daily paper ran an article about the case, but it only mentioned the guy who was making the phone calls. That eased my mind quite a bit. I kept looking online for anything that linked me to the episode, but nothing ever showed up. Dishearteningly, I did read some forum conversations about the incident, and the women who made comments were just flat out mean. They said things like: "Why are guys so f-ing creepy?" and "Good for you girls for reporting those dirtbags. They need to be taught a lesson." See? Where was the due process? The media painted a picture, and these people swallowed it hook, line, and sinker. I didn't know exactly what that other guy's story was, but I wasn't a dirtbag. It hurt to see those things written about me, even though I knew they weren't true. Once again, perception reared its ugly head at me.

44

Get Up

Given the state of mind I had been in before I found out about being reported to the police, you would think that being labeled a stalker might have pushed me over the edge. But somehow, in the depths of my despair, away from the sun, where the bitter cold went straight to my heart, something wonderful happened: I started to hear a familiar voice in my head, speaking softly. "Get up," it said. "Get up Darren." It was the same voice that had urged me through four hellish years in Veiltown. With that, the fighter inside of me, who had been knocked unconscious by a barrage that had lasted for the better part of five years, came to. There were still opportunities for peace all around me. There were good people that I could find solace in. It would be a long, hard journey back, but I couldn't give up. I remembered that all of the bad things that had gone on in my life recently, save my mother's passing, were because of choices I made. My lack of money, the loss of Gina's friendship, and even my new label as a stalker were due to me listening to my heart without regard for the suffering I might have to withstand. I made those decisions knowing full well what ills could befall me. I took chances so that I could look myself in the mirror and be able to say that I was a man of principle and conviction—never afraid to act when the circumstances necessitated. I did those things so that I might live truly, and in the process, truly live. It was time for me to take responsibility for my life and to find my way back into the sunlight. It was time to get right.

Since that time, I have started to get it together. I have realized that dentistry isn't so bad, at least for now while I need to get some of these debts paid off. I have developed great relationships with many of my patients, and I enjoy treating anyone who sits in my chair. I think they like me too. My search for places to work where I wouldn't feel at odds with the management has been rewarded with two more jobs: one doing hygiene near Beverly Hills once a week and another doing dentistry at a nonprofit clinic in the area, three days per week. I am a "half-time" employee at the nonprofit clinic, but I receive full medical and dental insurance coverage. That is something I have not had since I graduated from dental school. I couldn't afford it with all the crap I went through, and it was scary being without it, given how at any moment a serious accident can happen. I also receive quite a few more benefits, including paid vacation and sick days and paid dental continuing education courses. Plus, I work with an underserved community there, so I am happy to be contributing to the greater good. Not too shabby. I owe this job, for the second time, to Rachelle. Love ya girl.

I have also consolidated all of my student loans and taken most of my private debt to a debt management organization that will reduce it from thirty one thousand dollars to about twenty thousand. I will pay that off in three years max. I finished paying off my landlords from Laguna Beach too. With that out of the way and my three jobs, given some time, I am certain I will be able to get on top of my debts. It will take some discipline, but I'm up to it. I still don't want to be a dentist for too much longer, but I'll do my best for my patients while I get everything squared away. As for my future career? I've got some ideas...

My car eventually died on me. That used car dealership sure took me for a ride. Live and learn... I rode the bus for a few months afterwards because I couldn't afford to fix the darned thing at the time. Let me tell you, riding the bus as far as I had to is ridiculous. I got very little sleep because of it, and a lot of people on the bus smelled really bad. Nevertheless, I am glad that I had the opportunity to be reminded what real struggle is like. That helped me to realize that despite all I have lost, I have my health and an education and talent. Many of the people I saw on the bus aren't so lucky. They reminded me that I had better not mess this up. I don't have the right to.

As I mentioned before, Ansel and Wendy got married a while back. These last few months have seen Darren, Dustin, and Brendan get married as well. Darren even made me a groomsman. It was one of the greatest honors of my life to be such an important part of his brightest day, especially considering how relatively briefly we have known each other. DJ and Ayako have also become engaged, and so have Mara and her boyfriend of two years. I cannot express the pleasure it gives me to see my dearest friends find true love and a chance for happiness. In their fortune, my heart rejoices.

I think about my mother every day... For so long, I resented her for the way she played favorites with my sister and coddled me. Even so, I never doubted that she loved me. Some kids don't even have that. Even if she neglected to encourage me at times, I can't attribute it to any sort of malicious intent. At the worst, it could have only been inattention. And you know? I can't blame her. Her life was just as difficult as anyone's, and she had a lot of demons to beat back. It speaks to her character mightily that she was able to be such a loving person in the midst of such inner turmoil. Considering where she started, she didn't do too badly at all. She found love, and through everything, she kept it until her death. I am so glad that we had the chance to finally resolve our differences, Mom... I don't think I could live with myself if we hadn't. I love you.

45

What Does It All Mean?

As I look back, it is clear to me that even though I despised it, going to dental
school in Veiltown has helped me to grow immeasurably. Only as I have passed
further and further away from those times have I been able to comprehend the
extent to which they affected me. Only in retrospect can I even begin to
understand what I felt and thought while I was going through them. Once when
asked by a classmate what I had against Mason, I likened him to a "clumsy
puppy" who didn't know that what he was doing was wrong, so he just kept
doing it. I felt that Mason needed to be punished so that he would learn to stop
being so inconsiderate. As it turns out, regardless of my denials that I was
anything like Mason, I too was a "clumsy puppy," peeing on peoples' rugs, but
never being punished sternly enough to change my behavior or my thought
processes. I didn't understand how my openness and blunt honesty and
willingness to express my opinions could rightfully be considered offensive. I
was oblivious to the ways in which I affected others, and my life in Veiltown was
a lesson given to me so that I might grow. Growth takes perspective, to see what
we do wrong; courage, to accept it; and strength, to change it. My suffering

during dental school gave me perspective. I know now that I had not truly realized, while I was facing my trials in that city, just how thin the thread that I hung from was. Nor had I understood the extent of the damage that my isolated and downtrodden heart had sustained. Even without full realization, through those ills, I slowly began to stand in the mirror and to see the baser parts of my nature—to recognize the unwitting damage those parts of me could inflict on others. Even though a part of me hated those people for making me feel so rotten, I knew that I had to keep trying to see the good in them and the validity of their perspectives. Only with courage would I be able to accept my flaws: the courage to admit that I was the guilty party and that it was I who needed to change. The only way things could get better was through my own efforts to be more thoughtful, less self-concerned, kinder, gentler, better. Better… Only with strength to break my old, destructive habits could I move forward.

At first, I merely camouflaged my flaws. I chose not to be myself and devised an illusion to keep those around me content. Despite my façade, sometimes the truth would leak out to do its damage once more. I thought that I was doing everything right, and yet I couldn't gain the approval I yearned for. My heart became a tangled web of fear, anger, and sadness as I tried to no avail to blame others for my troubles while denying any wrongdoing myself. I created a shell to live in—a person who wasn't real. The more I failed, the more confused I became and the further I drifted away from who I really was. But at some point, acceptance of my flaws began to creep in. As I forced myself to see the truth, my habits started to change: gradually, but certainly. Instead of blaming others for my isolation, I started to ask, "What is my part in this? How can I be better so that others aren't disturbed by who I am and the things I do?" Then, instead of just acting considerate, I actually began to think about the feelings of others and how to avoid offending them during social interactions. I didn't think about how to avoid offending people for my sake only, but for their own sakes as well. It is difficult to change habits that one has developed over an entire lifetime, and at first, the going is slow. Even after I had started moving forward, doubt remained as to what I should say and how I should say it in order to show people that I was a worthwhile person and deserving of their respect. I was often afraid to say much because I didn't want to offend anyone. I found myself choosing not to say things that I probably could have, just for fear that people would think poorly of me. When I met C, I was in the beginning stages of my change, and I was at the same time both afraid to offend her and an open book in regards to how captivated I was by her. I held back my personality, but I couldn't hide my desire. How could she begin to see who I was? I didn't even know... Despite the setbacks, my growth continued forward, and I can truly say that I am a much better human being than I was when this all started.

The Merriam-Webster Collegiate Dictionary defines *stalk* as: "to pursue obsessively and to the point of harassment" ("²Stalk" ~*vt* def.3). I have already admitted that I was obsessed, and in that C obviously felt I was harassing her, I suppose I did "stalk" her, by this definition. Wikipedia.org states: "Stalking is a legal term for a pattern of offensive behavior involving repeated harassment or other forms of invasion of a person's privacy in a manner that causes fear to the target" ("Stalking"). The website goes on to explain that statutes for the behavior vary by jurisdiction but may include acts such as repeated physical following [I didn't do that], unwanted contact (by letter or other means of communication) [I did that], observing a person's actions closely for an extended period of time [I didn't do that], or contacting family members, friends, or associates inappropriately [sadly, I did that] ("Stalking"). Later, the article states that: "Contrary to crimes that consist of a single act, stalking consists of a series of actions which in themselves can be legal, such as calling on the phone, sending gifts [check!], or sending e-mails [check!]" (Sexual Harassment Support, 2006; as cited in "Stalking", 27 January 2008). On the American Journal of Psychiatry's website, the article "Study of Stalkers" identifies five types of stalkers: rejected, resentful, intimacy seekers, incompetent [suitors], and predatory stalkers (Mullen et al.). Out of these five groups, I had some of the characteristics of two of them: intimacy seeker and incompetent [suitor]. (Please visit the website for Sexual

Harassment Support at http://www.sexualharassmentsupport.org/
TypesofStalkers.html for detailed explanations) Even though I qualify as a stalker
when viewed in the context of the definitions and descriptions I chose to use here
(there are many others out there), I still don't perceive myself as one. True, I
exhibited some of the behaviors of a stalker, but I didn't exhibit many others. I
wouldn't have even qualified to be a subject in "Study of Stalkers" (Mullen et al.)
because I didn't meet the requisite amount of attempts at contact. (The study
called for subjects to have made ten attempts, and I only made four.) Also, as far
as I can discern, a stalker very often has some sort of diagnosable mental
disorder. I would bet money that if I took a battery of tests meant to determine
mental illness, not one would show a disorder of any kind. I'm not crazy… The
truth is that I was only reacting to a deep and burning need inside of me; my
heart told me to do something, and I listened. Still, the determination as to
whether or not someone is a stalker is largely based on the perception of the
victim. I did what I did, and C felt threatened by it. I can't deny that…

When I was getting my bachelor's degree in psychology, my teachers
were quick to point out the limitations and dangers of labels. I learned very
clearly that labeling a person has many unfortunate consequences. Most
importantly, it dehumanizes that person. It is easy for us as humans to use a small
tidbit of information to make a gross generalization about someone. It is also
unfair. Labeling someone as something such as a stalker or a murderer or even a
diabetic often eliminates the perceived need for others to learn more about that
person. The label becomes pervasive, and even if they don't intend to, others who
are unfamiliar with the individual often begin to define that person by just one
characteristic. When these people think of that person, they cannot do so without
connecting him or her to the label. A label such as "murderer" has an extremely
unfavorable connotation. Even if that "murderer" was completely justified in his
actions, on first contact, most people would automatically see him as an
aggressive, dangerous, bloodthirsty monster. A label such as "diabetic" might
lead people to believe that the labeled person is overweight and lazy. A label such

as "stalker" might give the impression that the person so labeled skulks around in the darkness and follows women home so he can watch them through their windows with binoculars. There is more to every person's story than what a label can tell you, and when you label people, you take away their credibility. You remove the value of their life, their struggles, and their humanity.

I can see now how I must have seemed to C. After our date and my response to her e-mail, there were no lines of communication, even after my best efforts to open one. Given the separation between us, it was only a foregone conclusion that I would become dehumanized to her. She couldn't see me as a person, nor did she want to. To her I became a mystery. With no clue to what my true intentions were, due to her unwillingness to actually look and see, C began to make unfounded assumptions that I was crazy and dangerous: a stalker. Now, whether I like it or not, to a certain group of women and one in particular, I am a stalker; and all of the reasons why I did the things I did are left irrelevant.

Human beings… What a beautiful disaster we are. What potential we hold—to love and to hate, to give and to take, to help and to hurt. A factor that makes all the difference in the paths we follow is our perception. If we chose to let our perceptions become negative by allowing them to be shaped by ignorance and assumptions, or by incomplete information, we follow a dangerous road. That road will often lead to the worst things in our nature: to fear and to anger, to spite and to vengeance. It can even lead to violence. However, if we struggle to shape our own perceptions by compassion and understanding and the will to appreciate the experiences and feelings of others, we follow a road to prosperity: to kindness and to service, to compromise and to love. I believe, after all I have been through, that it is not our place to expect the world to change for us. We cannot believe that others should go out of their ways to help us reconcile the discrepancies between the way we think the world should be and the way it really is; nor can we hide behind our pride and refuse to compromise, though our stubbornness might leave us huddled and shivering in dark shadows. We must take the initiative to shape our own perceptions favorably. I said in the introduction that perception has been one of the biggest problems in my life. I have finally realized that it was not the perceptions of others that caused my pain. It was my own perceptions that needed to change, and I am better for that realization.

I was driving just the other day, and I passed by a church. On the readerboard in front, there was a quote: "There isn't anyone you couldn't love, once you've heard his story." I smiled as I thought about what that means. One of the things that make us beautiful is our ability to understand what someone else is feeling: to put ourselves in another's shoes, so to speak. If we have the strength to get past our own selfish pride and apply this ability, it allows us to live outside of ourselves, if only for a moment. We can truly see what others see, feel their pain, and most importantly, accept and forgive. Everyone has a story, a past, a reason for the things they do; and it isn't hard to understand someone once we decide to try. If we open our eyes, our ears, and our minds, something magical happens. Something far greater opens: our hearts. It took me a long time to figure that out, but now I think I understand (although I still make mistakes from time to time). That is why, in spite of all of the sadness and anger and animosity that grew inside of me, I found a way to change myself and to have respect for the perceptions of others, even if I thought they were wrong; and that is why, even though my heart still bleeds for her, I won't risk another second of C worrying that I might be waiting around some corner to grab her. Even if in my heart I can never fully do so, at least in my actions, I have to let go of her. She has her reasons for not wanting to know me, and well… those reasons are good enough for me.

Through my ills, I have learned so many valuable lessons. Many of them have to do with the truths and illusions of the human condition. One of the most important things that I have taken from all of this is a newfound respect for the difficulty of the trials we all must face. Each and every one of us has problems; just because you might not be starving or have cancer, it doesn't make the things that you deal with in your heart and mind on a daily basis any less real. In my opinion, denying the validity of your own problems can only do you harm. I'm not saying you should catastrophize things that are inconsequential, but if something hurts you deep inside, you have to face it and explore it and do everything you can to resolve it. Feel the pain it causes you. Break down and cry; but do so with a fighting spirit, to cleanse yourself of all that torment. Let the sorrow of your missteps teach you to be better and to try harder: for yourself, but more importantly, for all the people who come into your life. Never forget that you are not alone in your search for clarity and redemption. We walk together. We rise, and we fall... together. Ultimately, we are all nothing more than lost children, searching for our way home and struggling desperately to hide our fear: fear of being hurt or ending up alone or just not being good enough. Only by leaning on each other can we truly understand: this self-inflicted suffering is merely an illusion put there to fool us into defeating ourselves and to stand in our way of peace. The true test of our existences is to rise above it—to overcome, even in the face of it. I believe that to do that, we must have love in our hearts: self love and love for others. These things will drive us forward, even at times when the strength to continue seems to have left us completely. They can light our way to a place where all of the troubles of our days fade away into bliss and serenity. Of this I am certain.

One day recently, a little girl and her mother came into one of the offices I work at to get their teeth cleaned. After I had finished with the little girl, she gave me a hug around my legs. She left the room as her mother settled with the receptionist, but then, a minute later, she walked back into the operatory and told me that she wanted to give me two more hugs. Smiling, I let her, making sure that she paused between the two so that they were distinctly separate. After she had gone, as I prepared the room for the next patient, I found I was having great difficulty holding back tears. That little girl was so trusting and loving. She was pure. It made me sad to think of the things we learn to do to each other and the terrible justifications we use in the process; but it also reminded me of the potential we have to love. To that little girl, I was worth something… just as we all should be to each other.

Truly, my road to hell was paved with good intentions. I never meant to cause any of the consternation that I did during those five years… to anyone. With that in mind, for my part, I offer my apologies and my forgiveness, especially to Mason, Kara, Renee, Liz, Steve, and Gina. Nonetheless, without making the mistakes that I did, I fear I would not have grown as much as I have. In retrospect, I can recognize so many things that I used to do wrong. I suppose the only way for me to learn not to do them was to face stern consequences, and I did. I lost so many things that mattered to me. I lost love. I lost respect. I lost direction. I lost friends… I even lost heart. But through the struggle, I somehow held together, even when the nights were so dark that I couldn't imagine seeing the daylight ever again. Undoubtedly, I couldn't have done so without all the special people who have been there to guide me through, even if I didn't mention some of them in this story. It goes without saying how thankful I am for each and every one of them.

As for C… Since the day that I took the last step—the one that finally and utterly separated me from any illusion that I might somehow find my way to her heart—dating has been difficult. For me, just knowing that she exists and trying to find the desire to be with someone else is something like trying to get excited about eating a fast-food cheeseburger after tasting filet mignon. It isn't as if I haven't had opportunities to date very beautiful women or women with great bodies or women with kind hearts or intelligent women. In fact, one woman I dated in particular was everything I could have ever wanted. I did have feelings for her, and she felt very strongly about me (which could only ever make me like a person more). In spite of the way she matched C in ways that I knew of, and perhaps was even better than her in ways that I didn't, she couldn't give me the butterflies that C could, simply by passing my way. C was the most beautiful light I ever saw, and the struggles I was going through when I met her only made her shine that much brighter. She was every love song I ever heard and the answer to the question. For her, I would have fought any battle or walked any distance. I still would. There's no limit to just how much I could have and would have gladly taken for her. (And I still have to scratch my head and smile at how powerfully she affected me, given the fact that I originally thought she was ugly. That has never happened to me before, and I doubt it ever will again.) I can't help but think that if I hadn't been so messed up in my heart and mind when I met her, things would have been different. Maybe it's just the manifestation of some internal defense mechanism, meant to justify what I put myself through, but I have to believe that. After all, Paige found me to be worthwhile once she got to know who I really was.

If I am to ever love romantically again, the woman will have to affect me at least as powerfully as C did, if not more so. And no, I'm not sure if that is possible. I am aware that with an outlook such as this, I am putting myself at great risk of ending up alone, but that is a cross that I am willing to bear. The reason is this: now that I know what I'm capable of feeling for someone and what I can give to the right woman, I can never in good conscience give less. It wouldn't be fair to do that to anyone. No one deserves to be settled for.

When I look back at all of it, I'd like to be able to say that I did this to myself. And I did, in some way. However, I cannot tell you that I had a choice. You see, choice falls within the realm of thought, but at the core of me, there was no thinking; there was only emotion, pure and raw. Though I tried for a time, I could no more temper it with logic than one could stop an avalanche with his hand or hold the ocean in a paper cup. My feelings for C were purely and utterly a product of who I was and who I am. It couldn't have been any other way. I never felt so alive as I did after I read her response to my letter, or so destroyed as I did the moment that she made it clear that we would not have a second date. But even though I ended up with a wound that runs so deep it may never completely heal, I am proud of myself for risking greatly, regardless of any fear of the consequences; because the consequences of failure are far less severe than the consequences of failure to act.

I guess sometimes in life, for whatever reason, we stand on the highest hill we can find and yell at the top of our lungs, just so someone will hear us. We believe that our words and what is in our hearts can make a difference: that our conviction is so strong, the sheer power of it can sway trees to uproot and persuade mountains to move out of the way. But there is never a guarantee that someone will hear our cries or that they will even be willing to listen. There is only hope… and I honestly can't think of something that we possess that is more important than hope.

I could fill another entire book with all the things I can say about C and the things I wish I could say to her. That would make for a rather long last chapter, so I will say just a few more things. In one of the letters that I wrote to C before I left Veiltown, but never sent, I felt as though I had captured the most convincing thing that I would ever be able to say to her. In the middle of a long, overly wordy paragraph in which I tried to explain why she should give me the chance to know her and to be with her, I wrote a sentence that summed up everything. It read: "If in your life, you were ever to kiss me, somewhere between thinking my heart was going to beat right out of my chest and wondering if you would ever be able to escape my arms, you would get it… you would understand." I don't know exactly what love is. In fact, as my life goes on, I become less and less sure. But one thing I am certain of is that love, if it is true, starts with a promise. That promise never has to be consciously made because it arises on its own, born for different reasons, unique to each of us. And yet, it really doesn't matter how or why it comes about: only that it is. I am sure—even though I cannot say I love C or ever did—that in the words written above, there was such a promise.

I have nothing left that has anything to do with C except for my poem on its scroll. Maybe I should have gotten rid of it, but I just haven't been able to bring myself to throw it away. It sits in my closet, in its golden tube, hidden from view behind some bags and boxes—a gift that will never be given. The price of keeping it? Every time I uncover it while looking for something else or when I move on to my next residence, I will be reminded: reminded of hope; reminded of the most unbearable sorrow and of the most incredible joy; the darkest nights and the brightest days; reminded of dances never danced, passion never received, and devotion never whispered; reminded of a promise never kept, and of a love never born; reminded... of a life never lived. And yet, without it all, I'm not sure if I would have regained what I had lost. Without C, I might not have remembered that I'm not dead; I'm still alive. My heart still beats and bleeds and yearns for a better tomorrow—something to look forward to. Because of her, I remember what passion feels like and I understand why I must have a similar passion for my life as its days come and go. In return, she will forever have my gratitude.

When I look in the mirror, in my eyes, I still see a shy little boy. As he has done for his entire life, he continues to swim boldly against the current. That little boy believes ever so strongly in more than just a normal life. He always has... He always will. All it took for him to remember was the most unlikely and unfortunate encounter with the most amazing woman. Thanks to her, that little boy once again believes in unimaginable happiness and in uncompromising love. Those things, he will always fight for, and the trials of the past few years have only strengthened his conviction. Through it all and in spite of it all, here I stand looking anxiously towards the future.

Why did I do what I did? Why did I keep trying? Why did I go so far? There are a million things I could offer as explanations, but behind all of them, there is only one real reason: unlike any woman I have ever met in my life, C was nothing less than magic. Magic like the sun rising over snowcapped mountains. Like eagles soaring or dolphins playing in the wake of an ocean liner. Magic... Magic like a touchdown pass from Joe Montana to Jerry Rice. Like Kerri Strug on vault in the 1996 Olympics. Like a three pointer at the buzzer. Magic like Christmas Morning. Magic like a litter of newborn puppies. Magic like a hug from Mom. Magic... like going home.

To C:

In all of this, my biggest regret is that I frightened you. For any anguish or frustration I ever caused, I apologize. May you find your way home and find it well.

THE END